Praise for *Secrets of Selling f*

It's an eye-opener! Every real estate sales agent and realty office manager should read and implement the outstanding techniques in this excellent new book. Terry Weaver shares his personal sales experiences gained over the years, plus techniques he learned from his students to create a unique "how to sell real estate" book. On my scale of 1 to 10, this superb new book rates a 10.
- San Francisco Examiner, April 2000

The powerful and practical material in this book has influenced my career more than anything else. It is now the first resource we require any person we hire in sales to read — and study!
- Jim Matoska, Vice President of Sales — The Ginn Companies

This is a superlative work. Terry Weaver has magically condensed a career of teaching into advice that will help anyone to become a more successful real estate salesperson... I urge all who are in real estate sales or thinking about it, to take it in ample doses.
- Jim Chaffin, Ace developer of Spring Island and Callawassie Island in South Carolina and Roaring Fork Club, Colorado; past president, Urban Land Institute

Everything Terry teaches and shares in this book has worked for me and many others I've known. He certainly gives you the tools. Use them wisely and you experience the true secrets of selling success.
- Brad Munday, Number one sales ace — Kiawah Island, South Carolina (for over 10 years)

The book helps to keep me between the lines. It reminds me of the things I've been doing right by confirming and refining my sales ability. Everyone, including the superstars, should read it regularly to stay on track!
- Kathy Iverson, Top Sales Ace, Slifer, Smith & Frampton; Vail Associates Real Estate

No one explains and teaches the real selling secrets better than Terry. This book will change your life if you let it — like it has dramatically changed mine!
- Glenn Cockrell — Antique Properties, Virginia (closes over 80% of prospects)

About the Author

As a native of China Grove, North Carolina, Terry cut his business teeth by selling books door-to-door for the Southwestern Company during summers between his years at the University of North Carolina. His extraordinary success earned him the company's number one position out of 7200 sales people in 1972. Upon graduation, he was hired as a sales manager and quickly established an enviable record, recruiting and training more than 1,000 successful salespeople.

In 1979, he made a career move into real estate on Hilton Head Island, South Carolina, where he established and maintained an impressive sales record. It led to his appointment as Director of Recruiting and Sales Training for The Sea Pines Real Estate Company.

Responding to constant requests for training services-both sales and management- Terry founded Master Sales Institute, Inc. in 1987- and the rest is history. In January of 2003 the company was renamed Marketing & Sales Institute, Inc. to better reflect the services it offers.

MSI focuses on sales and management training along with marketing consultation primarily for planned luxury communities. MSI also provides a national conference each new year known as ACES (Amenity Communities Excellence in Selling) attended by hundreds of sales and management executives from planned communities. Each year MSI also offers the Amenity Communities Marketing Summit, exclusively for Developers, Marketing Directors and Sales Managers.

Terry Weaver is member of the National Speakers Association and the Urban Land Institute. He resides in Hilton Head Island, South Carolina with his wonderful wife of over thirty years, Tillie.

SECRETS of SELLING
from
REAL ESTATE
MASTERS

SECRETS of SELLING from
from
REAL ESTATE
MASTERS

WHAT TOP PRODUCERS KNOW
THAT OTHERS DON'T

TERRY L. WEAVER

Published by Elevate, Charleston, South Carolina.
Member of Advantage Media Group.

ELEVATE is a registered trademark and the
Elevate colophon is a trademark of Advantage Media Group, Inc.

Printed in the United States of America

ISBN: 978-1-60194-001-8

Most Advantage Media Group titles are available at special quantity discounts for bulk purchases for sales promotions, premiums, fundraising, and educational use. Special versions or book excerpts can also be created to fit specific needs.

For more information, please write: Special Markets, Advantage Media Group, P.O. Box 272, Charleston, SC 29402 or call 1.866.775.1696.

DEDICATION

I have lived long enough to realize that I am today a mere product of all my yesterdays, and that my yesterdays were filled with influences of all those around me. How does one acknowledge and thank all of those who created such a lasting impact? Impossible! But it is possible to acknowledge the few who rise above the others. Thus it is that I dedicate this book to them.

To two ideal parents who brought me into this world and nurtured me through their example of unconditional love and integrity — Herman L. Weaver, who passed onto his final reward from the ordeal of Alzheimer's, March 28, 2001, and Margaret I. Weaver, who we lost suddenly to heart disease on July 15, 1998. I miss both of them so very much and look forward to seeing them.

To Tillie, who is the love of my life and mother to my two wonderful children, Ashley and Jason. She is the one who always stands by me, always believes in me, always encourages me, always accepts me.

To David Dean, a great manager of people, and a friend who always believed in me more than I did.

CONTENTS

Note: More information on Terry's training programs, along with how to order additional copies of the book, can be found following the final chapters. Also ask about the audio version of this book.

INTRODUCTION

This book has a very specific purpose. It has been designed and written to challenge and help stimulate your growth not only as a professional in our wonderful industry of sales, but personally as well. If the information contained in these pages only helps you make more money without helping you become a better person, then this book has been a failure. In other words, it is designed to challenge you and help you grow.

HOW DO WE GROW?

One of the main ways we can continue growing throughout our entire lives as long as our brains will function is through the collection and application of new ideas — through applied knowledge. Someone once said that knowledge is power. Do you believe that? I don't. Only *applied* knowledge is power.

Unused knowledge is worse than ignorance! At least an ignorant person has an excuse. You will be held more accountable after you read this book, so you had better not finish it if you want to be able to plead ignorance concerning how to sell in our communities because that excuse will be blown out of the water!

Over the years I've learned that if you boil the art of selling down to its most basic components, it can be expressed as the following equation:

Selling =
Educating *(your customer)* + **Motivating** *(your customer)*

The goal of this book is to educate and motivate *you,* as well.

I am going to give you from the initial interview through the closing of the sale and beyond, the step-by-step information you will need to become an ace at selling. I am also going to attempt to motivate you to accomplish this feat.

I think we all have a pretty good idea of what education is. If a student goes to college, does his homework, studies, absorbs the information, and later applies it in his profession, it could be said that he received a good education. Another student may have had the same professors and the same classes, yet he goes out every night and parties, copies homework, barely passes the exams, and slides through graduation. Did he get a good, quality education? Hardly, at least not in the areas for which the tuition was paid.

What's the difference between these two? Only that the first student took the *external information* offered by the professors and through discipline, study, and practice *internalized* the information so that it became true *education* to him.

MOTIVATION

Motivation is frequently more mysterious. One person can hear a speech, read an article or a book, observe a sunset or a heroic action like 9/11, and then go out and accomplish something great as a result of it. This person took external *inspiration,* internalized it, and converted it into *motivation.* Another person can see and hear exactly the same things and simply respond with a yawn, say, "That was nice," and then do nothing.

People change only because they choose to change. Most people do not choose to put forth the effort. The same external information and the same external inspiration are provided to different individuals, but are not internalized in the same way. The primary key to change is *desire.* What about you? Do you have that burning desire to change? Reading this book is a good indication that you do.

People are like sticks of dynamite: the power is on the inside. But dynamite is relatively worthless unless something happens on the outside. That fuse has to be lit. Sometimes it takes an external force, or a *spark* to ignite that internal resource or the explosive power that is there all the time.

The goal of this book is to provide that spark in your life. I have gleaned this information from more than thirty years of personal experience in sales and training. More than twenty of those have been in real estate. This is a compilation of data from many sales aces from around the country who surpassed me in the art of sales and who have unselfishly shared with me their knowledge of what works for them. Their help is greatly appreciated. They contributed to my growth and they can do the same for you.

This book contains words of inspiration. Some readers will respond with: "That's nice." My challenge to you is to not be one of those people. Take these words of inspiration, internalize them, and transform them into the motivation that will prompt you to take action to change and grow. Your job is to take this information, internalize it, and utilize it. Only you can transform it into education.

There was once a man in his mid-fifties who decided to retire. He said, "I'm going to retire early so that I can spend more time traveling, playing golf, and being with my grandchildren.

Unfortunately, none of his three able-bodied children had seen fit to bless him with grandchildren. He thought about it for a while and decided to provide some external incentive. He invited his children and their spouses to his house for a dinner party.

When they were all seated, he stood up at the head of the table and made the following announcement: "Family, I've decided to retire early so that I can spend more time traveling, more time playing golf and more time with my grandchildren.

"However, none of you have seen fit to bless me with grandchildren, so I've decided to place one million dollars cash into a trust fund that will immediately go to the first child of mine who blesses me with a grandchild.

"Now would you please bow your heads, close your eyes and let me ask the blessing over this food." He closed his eyes. He asked the blessing. He opened his eyes — and he was alone.

Yep, sometimes it takes an external force to ignite an internal resource that's already there!

Are *you* still with me?

A word of advice to you: If you want to be a high achiever, then force yourself to be easily inspired. Be soft and malleable like a warm piece of clay. Remember, our goal is *growth*. Growth is life. If you don't allow yourself to be inspired you automatically begin to expire, and something that is expired... well, you have the picture.

Plan your future carefully. You'll have to spend the rest of your life there.
— T. L. Weaver

1

TURNING POINTS IN LIFE

It's a funny thing about those turning points in our lives. We usually don't recognize them as such when we're in the middle of them, only when we look back years later.

In the fall of 1968 I was a freshman at the University of North Carolina. I arrived at one of those unforgettable turning points. A junior named Keith Valentine had come to U.N.C. from Wake Forest University to recruit students for the Southwestern Book Sales Company. He was trying to build a sales team to go out and sell a variety of books, the primary offering being a large, white family Bible that sold for $29.95.

I heard through a friend of mine that the recruiter was on campus. I looked him up. He came to my dorm room and explained the program to me. The idea of traveling to a different part of the country, meeting and dealing with all kinds of people, running my own business while being on my own and earning as much as I cared to from straight commission actually sounded a lot more intriguing than my previous summer jobs. I had loaded boxcars for the cotton mill, picked tomatoes, and made milkshakes. On the other hand, I was afraid of doing something I'd never done before.

Keith spent more than six long hours trying to convince me that it was a decision that I should make on my own if it was something that I wanted to do. I'd given him every objection in the book to put off making that decision, especially talking with my folks. Finally, he "closed" me.

When I went home and enthusiastically told my parents about this opportunity, they were anything but excited about it. In fact, my dad, being a very conservative banker, thought that the lack of guarantees and my having to pay all my own expenses was a harebrained idea. That's probably the very best thing he could have done because it gave me fuel for motivation. It gave me a cause. I had something to prove!

I began college with the desire to be a doctor. Chemistry helped me re-evaluate my goals in life. I didn't know exactly what I wanted to do, but selling books that summer opened my mind to all kinds of new possibilities. I sold with the Southwestern Company for five summers, knocking on doors from 8:00 in the morning until 9:30 at night for seventy-five hours per week.

It gave me the opportunity to meet over fifteen thousand people in a sales situation. I knew I had to knock on fifty to sixty doors every day in order to get into twenty-five homes. I needed to make my presentation at least twenty times in order to sell to five or six people. In less than thirty minutes, I had to establish rapport with a total stranger, convince them of their need for my product, and then close the transaction with a signed order and half deposit, all with just my word that I would bring their book back to them at the end of the summer before I went back to school.

Did I enjoy it? Hardly! Who would enjoy being rejected forty or fifty times a day? There were days when I sat in my car with tears in my eyes because of the frustration of it all.

Was the overall lesson in life valuable? It was the most valuable professional and personal experience I ever had in my life! It taught me lessons that I would have been hard pressed to learn in any other environment.

It taught me the power of persistence and just keeping on, even when I felt like giving up. It taught me the power of emotional control and forcing myself to act enthusiastically when I felt like crawling under a bush and crying. It taught me the importance of finding a way to succeed where others looked for an excuse to fail. It taught me that my success in life was going to be much more dependent on my attitude than on my aptitude.

After college I spent six more years with Southwestern as a district sales manager traveling to college campuses and offering students the same opportunity that I'd had. During that time I had the privilege of recruiting and training more than one thousand students.

You know, it's interesting that of the thousands of students I interviewed, rarely did I ever hear one of them say that they wanted to be in sales after graduation. Most of them had plans to be a doctor, lawyer, dentist, engineer, or accountant. You know, a professional.

We throw that term "professional" around a little too easily in our country. I can tell you that after thirty-plus years in business, "professional" has little to do with the profession and everything to do with the person who is in it. I've known garbage collectors who are more professional in their work than some doctors, lawyers and CEOs.

Frankly, I believe that if the product, the pricing, and the purpose is right, there is no greater profession than that of sales. If I weren't living out my lifelong dream as a professional speaker, marketing consultant, and sales trainer, I would be doing just what you are planning on, or are currently doing. I would be selling real estate in a beautiful community.

But like any other profession, it demands commitment. And before you can make a commitment, you need to know exactly why you're doing it.

WHY SELL REAL ESTATE?

Let's look at some of the most obvious advantages of this type of work. If you are considering this type of sales endeavor, perhaps this will push you over the edge. If you are already in it, then perhaps this will remind you of the reasons you chose it.

UNLIMITED INCOME POTENTIAL
If you want a raise in this business, it is not dependent on company politics, your tenure, or someone else's opinion of your work. You simply have a board meeting with the chairman while you are shaving or putting on makeup in the morning. You make up your mind that you are going to give yourself that raise by adjusting something in the way you are doing your business.

THE CHANCE TO BE YOUR OWN BOSS
Freedom! What a wonderful thing that is; however, most people can't deal with it. In fact, studies have shown that less than five percent of the U.S. workforce can work in an unsupervised capacity. Pitiful, huh? A much smaller percentage would even consider the possibility of working unsupervised on a straight commission basis. That takes a totally different type of person.

That's why *you* are so special. You maintain a tremendous amount of control over your own work schedule. In fact, this business gives you enough rope to either wrap yourself up a nice financial package, or hang yourself if you're not disciplined.

PRIDE IN YOUR PROFESSION
You are selling a worthwhile product, one that usually appreciates in value. You are providing a great service, whether selling in a primary or second home market. You are helping people's dreams come true. You are providing a great deal of service to the customers who buy from you. The vast majority of them will thank you years after they've purchased.

RUNNING YOUR OWN BUSINESS
Selling in this type of industry gives you an unlimited upside potential financial gain, with very limited downside risk. Compare our business to the cost of setting up a retail business — hundreds of thousands of dollars up front, signed leases, purchasing trips, dealing with employees — and *man,* is it hard to find good employees! And even with that, the odds of failure are quite high. Even the businesses that survive generally show no profit for at least the first three years.

MINIMAL INITIAL INVESTMENT
Think about the commitment of time, energy and money needed on the front end of our business compared to that needed for becoming a doctor, lawyer, or dentist. If you are truly committed to being a sales ace, there will be years of continued learning and practicing the skills of persuasion, but you still get to earn a super income while you learn.

BUILDING GENUINE JOB SECURITY
There is only one place you can build true security when it comes to your work, and that is inside yourself. Most people tend to put their trust in their job, the position, the company. If that job is lost, then unfortunately, there goes their security.

You're different. You have the opportunity to develop one of the most marketable skills possible regardless of the economy's ups and downs. You're developing the skill of persuasion.

Talk about security! If you are good at the art of persuasion, you can write your own ticket and acquire a position anywhere in the country, or even the world. Now, *that's* job security!

THE "BIG BUCKS"

Were you attracted to the job because of the potential "big bucks"? That's fine if you have a good philosophy of money. Keep in mind, though, that you don't *make* money. The Bureau of Printing and Engraving does that. You *earn* money as an exchange for services rendered.

Let me ask you a question: Have you determined your philosophy of money?

I determined my philosophy when I was around twenty-five years old. I decided that rather than work pretty hard for forty-plus years and then maybe have enough to retire on, I would rather pay a much bigger price on the front end. It made sense to me to work really hard in an industry in which high income was possible. And then by controlling my expenditures, for the remainder of my life I would be able to have something few are able to enjoy: *financial freedom.*

For me money is not for power, influence, prestige, or to fill an emptiness inside (because I guarantee you that it won't). Rather, money helps provide freedom, peace of mind, and not being a slave to what I can or cannot afford to do. Looking back over twenty-five years, I have learned that it was a wise decision.

I would encourage you to decide what money represents to you. Doing so will add energy to help you pay the price and endure the emotional valleys to get it.

If you are going to be good at this career, you have to make the commitment to do what it takes. You are the only one who really knows. Are you ready to make that commitment?

DO YOU HAVE THE RIGHT STUFF?

Do you have what it takes not only to survive but to thrive in this business? Intelligence, likable personality, personal appearance, a reasonable amount of class — sure, all those things are helpful. But all of them pale in comparison to one essential attribute: *commitment.*

Commitment is the ingredient sorely lacking in our country today, both professionally and personally.

Back during those book-selling days I watched many red-blooded all-American kids, often those with high profiles on campus such as the fraternity and sorority presidents or the captains of athletic teams, go through a commitment ceremony before being sent to their territory to sell. They vowed to stick it out and do the very best they could for the entire summer. Then they would go out, try it for a few days or maybe a couple of weeks, and then quit!

How could they do it? How could they face their dads or moms? Beats me!

That great Italian philosopher and football coach Vince Lombardi once stated, "Winning is a habit. Unfortunately, so is losing." Well, quitting can easily become a habit, too.

Let me encourage you to accept something right up front. If you are new to the business you will learn it quickly, and if you are experienced you already know it. You don't *try* real estate sales, *it tries you!*

How many people pay the price to get into medical school to simply "try" being a doctor? Or go to law school to "try" being a lawyer? Sure, a few do, but the ones who make great strides, the ones who succeed at the highest levels, are the ones who, like sales aces, see their work as a career and not just a job.

Like an ace fighter pilot, it becomes a mission, not just a position. It is a challenge, not just the means to a check.

Don't say, "Well, I'll make it if everything works out." Everything won't work out, I can guarantee it. Don't say, "I'll see if I like it." You won't like it some of the time — that's why they call it work. Don't say, "If marketing brings in enough prospects, I'll do just fine." Forget it! Don't base your success on someone else's efforts. Become your own marketing department if you have to.

Two guys were stuck on a roof in the middle of a flood. One of the guys pointed excitedly to a hat floating on the water. It would float down about thirty yards and then stop and come back. "What's that hat doing floating back and forth?"

The other man said, "Oh, that's just Uncle Charlie. He said he was going to cut the grass come hell or high water!"

In real estate sales you'll probably experience both of these — hell and high water — at some time or another. If you're going to be a success in this business, you have to be as committed as Uncle Charlie.

WELCOME HOME

Oh yes, back to my introduction to selling. That first summer selling books was quite a challenge for me. In fact, it was the biggest that I'd ever faced up until that point. At times every fiber in my being wanted to quit and go home, but I couldn't.

Then it was August 1969. The first summer of banging on doors had finally ended. Leaving Ohio, I headed back to Nashville to the home office to pick up my check for my summer's savings. It was going right into my account for school.

I called home to tell my folks that I would arrive in abut ten hours. I will never forget that feeling inside as I drove that old dusty '63 Ford Galaxy up that country dirt road to my home in China Grove, North Carolina. I pulled into the driveway and there stood the whole family waiting for me, almost like I was coming home from war.

Actually it was a war — a war with my own emotions. My mom walked over to me and gave me a big hug and kiss. My two sisters and my girlfriend did the same. The cat wove around my legs and the dog wagged all over. My dad was just standing quietly by himself over to the side. I walked over to him and stuck out my hand.

He shook it, looked me straight in the eye and said, "Good to have you home, Son. How'd you do?"

"Well, Dad, my goal was to make about seventeen hundred dollars this summer to pay for my own tuition because that's what the guy said I could do. But it didn't turn out quite like I planned."

"That's okay, Son," said Dad. "We'll still love you. How'd you do?"

I reached into my wallet and pulled out my check and handed it to my dad. He looked at it, looked back up at me, and looked back down at it again. He was probably counting the zeroes — because the check was for $4000.23!

He looked up at me again, this time with tears in his eyes. He shook my hand again, squeezing it a little harder, and said, "Welcome home, Son. I'm mighty proud of you!"

Then he slowly turned and walked inside the house. That's all he needed to say. Just those few words from him made every slammed door, every hundred-degree day, every seventy-five-hour week, every rejection all worth it.

By the way, Keith Valentine's persistence, until 2:30 A.M. that first night, persuading me to take the challenge, was indeed a turning point in my life. He wouldn't take no for an answer and I gave him a lot of excuses he had to overcome.

Looking back more than thirty years later, I can say that it was one of the most important decisions of my life. Thanks, Keith!

Low-paying is any job that has money as the only motivation for doing it.
— T. L. Weaver

$$2$$

CLIMBING INSIDE YOUR BUYER'S HEAD

Any war general will tell you that one of the most important things in winning a battle is to know your enemy. In fact, Napoleon said, "Winning a war is 90 percent knowledge." All championship athletic teams watch their opponents time and again on game films in order to determine the way they think, the way they act, the way they react, and to discover their weakness. If you are learning to fly, one of the things the instructor will teach you is about what is going on inside of the clouds. You must realize that there are certain "clouds" inside of the buyer's head as well. And you must learn to navigate around or through them.

Any superstar company of sales and marketing will spend lots of money and time on customer research. They want to ascertain an accurate buyer's profile. Computer companies, car companies, athletic equipment companies, etc., all know more about the buyers' habits than the buyers themselves. That's one of the things that make them so successful. They understand the exact target they are aiming for.

UNDERSTANDING THE BUYER

One of the best ways we can begin learning about our buyers is to first analyze ourselves. Most human beings have a lot of similarities. How do you buy something? What is it that takes you from being totally ignorant about a product to becoming an excited owner and user? Think about one of your last major purchases. Maybe it was a car, a nice stereo or even real estate.

Let me explain to you how this transaction actually took place. I challenge you to read the seven steps; think carefully to see if they don't ring true in your mind concerning your own purchasing experience.

A tremendous amount of marketing dollars are aimed at those who have already purchased. Sounds strange, huh? Why does this happen? It is because companies realize that once a customer is convinced that he made a wise choice, nothing can come close to the power and influence of word-of-mouth advertising. They want to create a fanatical convert in order to have a major marketer. After you've made a major purchase, don't you find yourself noticing the ads and reassuring yourself, "Yep, I sure made a good choice on that"?

You may not have been conscious of exactly what happened during this purchasing process, but these seven steps moved you from non-owner to owner. Pick up any magazine or newspaper, or turn on the TV and observe the ads. Pay attention to the grab lines. Billions of dollars are spent on these lines which are carefully designed to accomplish one purpose: *to grab your attention*. They want you to think. They want your response to be, "Hey, maybe that's what I need," or "That sounds really good!"

Once they've grabbed your attention, they have a second goal: *to breed discontent*. The superstar company realizes that if you are totally content with your current product, then you have no real reason to switch or upgrade. They realize that they must convince you that with their product that you will look better, smell better, feel better, be more popular, or whatever. Our entire economy is built on the concept of breeding discontent.

COMPANY'S GOAL	PROSPECT'S ACTION AND RESPONSE
Must *captivate* target market's attention.	You saw an ad, or a friend told you.
Must *cultivate* curiosity in the prospect's mind.	You begin wondering if this product or service may have some appeal to you.
Must *activate* recognition for the need or want of the product.	You start thinking about this idea and become discontent with your current situation.
Must *stimulate* active research on the prospect's part.	You begin looking into the claims and benefits of this product or service (internet, *Consumer Reports*, friends' opinions ...).
Must *educate* about the factual features of the product.	You realize there are enough attractive points that ignite sincere interest in your mind.
Must *motivate* with the emotional benefits that the product offers.	Your mental interest turns into emotional desire based upon the belief that this product will enhance your life by alleviating pain or by adding pleasure.
Must *eliminate* buyer's remorse for choosing that particular product.	A superstar company will follow through with phone calls and mailers coupled with superb service hoping to head off any doubts about your purchase being a wise decision. They know that a fully satisfied and excited owner is their best means of marketing.

THE DIFFERENCE BETWEEN MARKETING AND SELLING

There is a vast difference between marketing a product or service and selling it. Marketing's primary goal is to generate a bona fide prospect. In fact, marketing consists of the first four steps of the previous seven. Take another look at them.

The next three steps involve the primary responsibility of sales. Marketing and sales have to work hand in hand to accomplish the seventh step, which is eliminating buyer's remorse. Since the primary focus of this book is on the *selling* of real estate, not on getting listings, let's learn what must be done to become a sales ace. If the goal of marketing is to *generate a prospect,* then the goal of sales is to *convert the prospect into a customer.* These lessons of selling, however, should be used in dealing with sellers, too. After all, aren't you trying to persuade (sell) the owner to list with you?

PSYCHOLOGICAL PATH OF THE BUYING PROCESS

All buyers must take a mental and emotional journey down that buying path. Here's how you can help them along.

Empathy. This is rare for most salespeople. To best understand how to sell the product, we must first understand what is going on inside that customer's head. It has been wisely said that "To know what Jim Smith buys, try seeing it through Jim Smith's eyes." Makes sense to me.

We discussed a little about marketing efforts, so now let's look at your responsibility as the sales ace. Consider your brain and how it functions. It is probably the least understood organ in the entire human body. It is what happens inside this organ that converts prospects into customers. We have one brain, but it's divided into two hemispheres. Each of these seems to have its own distinct functions. They almost operate independently of each other. The left side of the brain tends to be the more analytical, problem-solving, and logical side. The right side tends to deal more with the imagination, humor, and the emotions.

Everyone receives input from both the right and left sides of the brain. Consequently, your presentation must address both sides to be successful in the selling of your community. Remember, if you are in sales, your two primary functions are educating your prospect and motivating your prospect.

Study the following progressive diagram of what takes place inside the prospect. Then we will look at it piece by piece for a clearer understanding. To refine your selling process, we must first define the selling process.

THE PSYCHOLOGICAL PATH OF THE BUYING PROCESS

Selling Involves ...

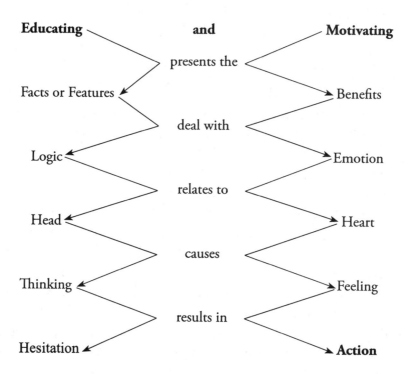

(Refer to this chart as you read its explanation.)

Educating teaches the prospect what the product has, or the specific features that it offers.

Motivating speaks to a deeper level of what the product has — for the prospect, or how he or she will *benefit* as a result of this particular feature. Most salespeople are quite adept at pointing out features, but often drop the ball by not piggybacking the facts and features with the emotional benefits. They just assume that these benefits will automatically flash into the prospect's mind. That's a costly and dangerous assumption. *People will see in their minds what you say with your mouth.* Look at the following example of speaking to a couple with a small child:

Feature: "The next home we're going to see is on the very end of a cul-de-sac…" (So what?!)

Benefit: "…so little Ralphie will be able to play outside on his Big Wheel away from traffic without your having to worry about his safety."

Facts or features deal with logic, which relates to the head. **Benefits** deal with emotions relating to the heart. Does this mean that the fist-sized pump inside the buyer's chest has something to do with buying real estate?

No! It's a different heart. The word "heart" is well over three thousand years old and comes from the ancient Greek word for "bowels" or "intestines." Do we not express a deep feeling by saying, "I feel it in my gut"? We Americanized it (probably Hallmark) just to sell cards!

I was driving down the highway and happened to notice a billboard advertising the United Way: "Open up your heart and give." What do they really mean by that? They realized that if they could get you to open up your heart — that treasure chest containing your emotions — then getting you to open your wallet would be no problem. The same thing happens with selling real estate.

Why does educating lead to *hesitation,* and motivating lead to *action?* As long as we have a bunch of facts bouncing around inside our heads, we won't make a decision if we feel we need to think about it some more. But if something "just feels right," then, and only then, do we move on with it. Most salespeople are much better at educating their prospects than they are at motivating them. They take the time to learn the product — the square footage of the house, the length of the golf course, the homeowner fees, etc., but they take little time studying and understanding human nature and what motivates people to make large purchases.

CREATING OBJECTIONS FOR OURSELVES

Keep in mind that your presentation must be balanced. If you thoroughly educate the prospects but do a poor job of motivating, then you have created *information overload.* The natural objection would be, "We just need to think about it." How many times have you heard: "You sure are a good salesperson. You've given me a lot to *think* about. I'll have to *think* about it and get back with you in a few days"?

By the way, that is not a compliment! When you hear a statement like that, you ought to smack your head! Because if they feel they are being *sold* on something, then there is something wrong. What they are really saying to you is, "I can tell that you want to sell something and that you know your stuff, but I don't sense any real desire on your part to help me experience any of the feelings about what owning here would be like." Then, they will thank you, leave you, and get hooked up with some other salesperson who understands how to motivate them emotionally. They will buy from him or her, which will just blow your mind! And you did a lot of the work. Only you just did it for free!

On the other hand, if you get your prospect all hyped up and excited without educating him on why it makes good sense to do what he is thinking of doing, he may go up like a Fourth of July rocket and commit today but cancel tomorrow due to a lack of intellectual confidence in making a wise decision. You have to remember that **people make buying choices based on what motivates them — the emotion — but justify that choice based on the facts that educated them and made logical sense.**

DIFFERENT MOTIVES FOR DIFFERENT PEOPLE

It is hard enough just trying to motivate people to do something that you would like them to do, but it is nearly impossible to do so a consistent basis unless you understand what that person's motivations are. Different people have different motives for purchasing real estate. That is the reason that selling is an *art*, not a science. People have different needs, different wants, and different backgrounds. One of the most important keys to becoming successful in selling is to develop strong listening and observation skills, like a good detective. During the initial meeting with the prospects, observe their behavior, their openness (or lack thereof), their dress, their questions, and listen to the way they answer questions.

Even though people are different, their motivations for making a purchase seem to fall into seven different categories called *dominant buying motives:*

- desire for physical security and safety
- desire for financial security and potential gain
- desire for social acceptance and the need for friends

- ego fulfillment, personal recognition, and gratification
- desire for comfort, enjoyment, and absence of pain
- desire for happiness
- family welfare and closeness; building memories.

Even though the decision to purchase is usually based on a combination of a couple of these different motivations, most of the time there tends to be one or two dominant buying motives.

During my years of selling real estate on Hilton Head Island, South Carolina, I learned the business the way most real estate agents learn it: by trial and error, with error accounting for a lot of lost commission dollars and un-helped people.

IT ALL STARTS WITH KNOWLEDGE

The older I get, the more I realize there is but one wealth, one security, on this earth and it is found in the ability to perform a task well. First and foremost, this ability must start with knowledge.

— Abraham Lincoln

The vast majority of real estate professionals have never really been trained in how to sell. Just compare what it takes to sell in our industry to that of other companies.

A friend of mine, Bob Porter, sold real estate for years for the Sea Pines Real Estate Company. He had been the senior vice president of marketing for Johnson & Johnson and had managed salespeople who sold surgical supplies to surgeons while they were in the middle of operations. The salespeople had to know human anatomy as well as how their products would be better than what the surgeons were currently using.

Bob told me, "Terry, before our salespeople could make calls on these surgeons, they had to memorize one hundred and twenty pages and understand what they were doing."

Major insurance companies such as Northwestern and Mutual of New York require that their salespeople undergo stringent and regular training in sales so that they understand how to sell the benefits of their programs and overcome the objections they may encounter.

What do we do in our industry to prepare a person for the license to practice? Most states require a meager thirty-hour course or maybe sixty hours that focus on what they must believe are the essentials of our business, such as fiduciary relationships and what it means, agency disclosure, radon gas, and lead paint laws.

Then a student takes a "multiple guess" test, and if he or she gets 70 percent right, voila! Out walks a "professional" real estate agent who will counsel individuals on possibly the most expensive product they will ever purchase.

Is that absurd or what?! The real estate license contributes to your success in selling real estate about as much as a marriage license does in building a relationship.

Then, with license in hand, the search begins for a broker's office in which to hang it. Typically, the broker shakes hands with the novice agent, and says, with congratulations, "Here is your desk. Here is your phone. Get to work. You're on your own!" After about six months, it's not only the license the new agent wants to hang!

And yet we wonder why our industry has a 50 percent attrition rate within the first twelve months and nearly 80 percent within two years!

OPTIMAL ORDER OF EVERY SALE

Before you will ever be proficient as a real estate sales ace, you must understand the basics of salesmanship. There is an ideal order for every sale regardless of product or service, and understanding this optimal order will greatly increase your odds for success. This order is as follows:

- the greeting and approach
- the initial office interview/overview
- the discovery presentation
- the closing for a decision.

These basics hold true whether you are selling books door-to-door or a waterfront million-dollar home.

What follows may seem quite elementary. I hope that I have succeeded in making these complicated steps sound simple. But their proper execution is quite involved and determines the difference between a sales disgrace and a sales ace.

Twenty-five years later, I just wish I could have had the information in my hands that you hold in yours today. What a difference it would have made! Let it do that for you — now!

3

THE GREETING AND APPROACH

Every good sprinter knows that one of the most important aspects of winning a race is the way he or she starts. In fact, at a track meet, you can watch as the sprinters adjust their starting block, shoot off like a rocket for four or five strides, come back and start again. So...

Get ready, get set, STOP!

Much like a sprinter, the way we start our day has much to do with the way we finish it. It is important to *get ready* for the day by dressing properly to know that you look like the professional you say you are. And it is easier to feel good when you know you look good. Sure, it's important to get your day set for what you want to accomplish. But before you go, *stop!*

It is important to get your spirit right. Your spirit is the true, deep you. Let me encourage you to accept a word of advice. I learned this back during my book-selling days. It is something that has helped me tremendously for thirty years. Rather than rush out of the house all frazzled and in a state of panic, find a quiet place where you can be alone with your thoughts. Spend at least twenty minutes reading some inspirational material.

Take your mind off *making a living* and instead put your mind on *living.* There are tools for helping you do this. Most important would be the Bible (especially Proverbs) or the religious book of your choice that will help you center your thoughts on living. One such helpful book is *Come before Winter* or *Growing Strong in Seasons of Life* by Chuck Swindoll. Or try books by Norman Vincent Peale or Robert Schuler. As you read, think about the direction your life is taking. And think of all you have to be thankful for. Think about your purpose for doing what you are doing.

The next step is for you to think about how you can better serve your loved ones, friends, and customers. Think about the priceless gift of a new day and how to make it better than the irretrievable yesterdays. Then, with your body, your external appearance, and your internal motivation (your mind and spirit) in place, you are ready to face the day.

Now, let's go to the office….

The first thing you need to realize is that just about everyone who walks into your office is experiencing a degree of apprehension and even fear. One of your main goals is to put them at ease and to capture their attention. Actually, you will get their attention whether you realize it or not, and it can either be in a negative of positive way. We have all heard the phrase that "you do not get a second chance to make a good first impression."

Indeed, it is the little things that we do (or don't do) that can make a big difference.

THE GREETING

The sales office should be bright and open, and present a neat and orderly appearance. Photographs representing the different activities and lifestyles in your community should be displayed all around the office on the walls. These photographs should show people engaging in activities in your community in exactly the way you want your community represented. Not just a photo of the lake, but people actually fishing on it. Not just observing a waterfall, but people picnicking beside it. Real owners beat stock models. Below the picture have a strong quote from the actual people in the photographs.

On one side, have a regional location map with your community in the center of concentric circles that indicate driving time to various spots such as the beach, the mountains, the hospitals, schools, shops, and the downtown area. On both sides of the location map should be large photographs of two or three of the main attractions of your community. They might be of the marina or an outstanding hole of golf or the clubhouse.

If the size and arrangement of your personal office is not conducive to sitting down with two or three people and conducting the initial interview, then the sales center should have several conversation pits where this can take place in relative privacy. These may be sections that are separated by half-walls or planters, or even a round table on the back deck. Just make it somewhere you can comfortably sit down and go through a good diagnostic initial interview.

The sales center should be attractive to the senses. There might be soft classical music playing in the background. One of the best sales centers I have ever experienced is at Eagle Harbor, just outside of Jacksonville, Florida. It always has popcorn popping or chocolate chip cookies baking which obviously creates a welcoming atmosphere when people walk in. It gets me going just to stand there and breathe.

THE APPROACH

As the prospects walk in, they should be greeted by a sincere, friendly, smiling, well-trained person at the front desk. Too much money has been invested to get these prospects this far to have them feel turned off by the person at the front desk.

Key points for the receptionist:

- The front desk person should immediately stand and acknowledge the prospect's presence with a wave, a nod, and a smile, even if he/ she is talking on the phone.
- When not on the phone, the receptionist should stand to greet the prospects.
- Let the prospect make the first move toward a handshake.
- The receptionist should be smartly attired and present him/herself with a smile and a friendly, upbeat greeting.

Here's an example:

Receptionist: "Good morning! I'm Ruby. Welcome to Eagle's Roost. How may I help you?"

Prospect: "Just wanted a little information about your community."

Receptionist: "Well, we are glad you're here. If I could get your help for just a minute to fill out our registration card, it will help us to provide better service to you while you're here. While you are doing that I will be glad to get Jenni to help you."

Please note that if Ruby did this correctly, she referred to you by name, not as "an agent" or "a sales executive."

WORDS CAN MAKE OR BREAK YOU

As a sales professional the most powerful tool you have at your disposal is the proper use of words, yet all across the country I find real estate people using some of the worst industry jargon to describe the products they are trying to sell. Let's study a few examples.

Unit. How many times have you heard a home or condominium referred to as a "unit?" What is a unit, anyway? It creates no positive emotional feelings, does it? Psychological studies have shown that the number two word for creating emotion is the word *home. (Mother* is number one.)

I don't imagine you got excited years ago when your parents told you, "Kids, we're going to Grandma and Grandpa's unit for Christmas." And how many times have you ever seen an owner display with pride a plaque on their wall that says "Unit, Sweet Unit." Remember the first time you went away from your family for any length of time, perhaps to summer camp or college? Did you ever feel unit-sick? I don't think so!

Lot. This is also a term to avoid for the same reason. What is the image of a lot? It may be a vacant piece of land in the middle of a city with broken glass, rusted cans, and probably used needles lying around. It's where we park our cars. It's not quite what our prospects want, is it? They want a *homesite.* It paints the proper picture.

Deal. We don't put together a "deal." We don't want to cheapen our offer. It's a *transaction.* Or a chance to take advantage of an opportunity.

Price. We tend to tell people about the "price" of our product. Price indicates cost, an expense, or something that we are giving up, such as "paying the price." We shouldn't use words that imply loss.

Instead, we should use a word that is attractive to people, like the word *value.* After all, that's what people want to buy, isn't it? Think about your community or a similar one that has been around for more than five years. Is it more expensive to buy today? Values have increased.

More words to avoid:

Project. Unless you are selling government housing, I hardly think that you are selling a project. Yet how often do we refer to it as that? People don't want to live in a project, they want to be in a *community.* They don't want to be in a development or a subdivision. Speak in terms of what they're trying to create. They want to be in a *neighborhood.* Can you see the late Mr. Rogers starting his show by saying, "It's a beautiful day in the project"? I don't think so!

Guard gate. If people wanted to be guarded they would be in the penitentiary. What they want is to feel secure, so why not paint that picture? Let's call it a *security gate,* or checkpoint, or a filter that keeps those out who are not supposed to be in. It's the same with the person who works the gate. He or she is best called a *security officer,* unless you happen to be selling at a prison.

Restrictive covenants. Real estate purchasers are quite independent in their thinking, and the last thing they want to be is restricted. What they do want is to be protected. They want their future values protected; therefore, we have *protective covenants.*

Decision. Most people hate to make them. Can you imagine walking up to Baskin & Robbins and seeing a sign that reads: "31 Decisions"?! People would rather have *choices.*

Spec house. I don't know of any owner whose chest swells with pride when receiving a compliment from their first guest in a new home and says, "Yeah, it was a spec."

"Spec" sounds like leftovers from a fly! People are, however, proud owners of a *model,* a *showcase home,* or a *builder's featured home* (featuring the quality of his construction).

There are also some phrases that should be avoided entirely, such as the following responses to a prospect's question: "That's a good question. Let me be honest with you," or, "May I really level with you?"

What kind of thoughts might go through the prospect's mind on hearing one of these? Perhaps, "Funny, I thought he had been leveling with me the last three hours." Why plant those seeds of doubt?

Sell/sold. When dealing with a prospective buyer, we should never use the words "sell" or "sold." It's a basic premise about human nature: People hate to be sold. But they love to *buy*. In fact, any overt attempt to sell will simply create a resistance to buy. Instead they *bought, selected, got involved, purchased.*

It makes sense then that when the receptionist refers to you that she does so by your name, not as a "salesperson" or a "sales agent."

REMEMBER NAMES

If at all possible, the receptionist should take the registration card back to the next agent on duty. (Hey, that's you!)

When you get the card, don't just grab it and run. Pause for a few moments before going out to meet the prospects. Look at the names and say them out loud to yourself. Make sure you have a reasonably correct pronunciation of the names, first and last. In Dale Carnegie's book *How to Win Friends and Influence People,* he states, "A person's name is the sweetest sound to his ear." I actually still see salespeople who have never read that all-important book!

Notice where they are from. If you have a moment, recall any other owners you may have from that same area. You may have an owner's guide that you can check quickly. Remember these people as you move into the initial interview.

Now take a couple of deep breaths and relax, even if you've just hung up from receiving bad news on the phone. Remind yourself: "There's nothing I can do about that now and I am not going to let the past control what happens to me in the future." Tell yourself, **"It's show time!"**

Give these people all of your focus. Warm up that smile and practice that professional attitude. Remember you are the one in charge.

You must create a casual and yet professional impression. Your countenance needs to reflect the lifestyle you're selling. Your attire needs to be sharp and crisp but not too dressy, especially if you're selling a community with a relaxed lifestyle.

You want to get on a first-name basis as soon you comfortably can, but use your own judgment about this by evaluating their openness, receptiveness, and age difference. If it is obvious that there is a substantial age difference between you and the prospects, it is much better to be on the conservative side and refer to them as "Mr. and Mrs." until you get their implied or direct permission to do otherwise. If you see that a person is a doctor or involved in the military, keep in mind that Dr. or Major *is* their first name. They worked long and hard to get that title and they expect you to recognize it.

If you have the registration card in hand before coming out, call them by name as you approach.

Jenni: "Hi there. Jason and Ashley Johnson? I am Jenni, Jenni Smith. Welcome to Eagle's Roost! How may I help you today?"

Prospect: "We just wanted to get a little information from you. We don't have a whole lot of time."

Jenni: "Well, I certainly appreciate your coming in. Why don't you step over here and I'll be glad to help you with that."

Accustom yourself to using their names throughout your entire time with them. Don't overuse their names, though. It can make you come across as being rather phony.

You may be saying to yourself, "I'm horrible at remembering names." Welcome to the world of the majority! Here are two suggestions for you:

First, don't trust your memory. Write down the name on a pad or make sure both names are on the registration card. Have you ever been with people for a couple of hours in the car, looked over to your right at the person sitting beside you and then felt panic gripping your guts as you thought, "What in the world is his name?"

Then you just hoped and prayed that his wife would mention it. That's rather dangerous because you wouldn't want to call him "Honey" or "Sugar." (That may not go over real well!) Spare yourself that embarrassment. Write it down! And keep it with you!

Stop confessing about how bad you are with names. We often end up possessing what we keep on confessing. If we say it so much, we literally convince ourselves of it.

When you are meeting someone without a registration card and you are hearing their name for the first time, focus all of your mental energies on that person. Wade Shealy is a topnotch sales professional. He says that when he first meets someone, he pretends that he has elephant ears that reach out and wrap around that individual, blocking out any type of external interference. As you give your name and listen to theirs, do the following:

- Make sure you hear it correctly!
- If it is an unusual name then ask them to spell it. They will be impressed that you even care.
- Repeat the name as you ask, "How may I help you, Jim?"

As they are answering the question, this is one time that you can cheat a little on listening to their answer. Instead, you should be repeating their names to yourself in your mind as you see their names running through your brain like a ticker tape or a flashing neon sign over their heads. Some names can be associated with a certain experience or someone else you know. In fact, the crazier and more ridiculous the association, the easier it is for your mind to lock onto it and remember it. Keep in mind, though, that you're only trying to remember it for a minute or so until you can move them out of the greeting area over to a place where you can comfortably jot it down on paper.

NOW SMILE AND TAKE CONTROL

When you greet them for the first time and exchange names, show them a warm, friendly, and sincere smile — not a grin from the teeth out, but a smile that comes from deep down inside.

Jim Coleman, a successful developer, was a real estate sales ace for at least a dozen years on Hilton Head. He said that as he approached his prospects for the first time he would think to himself while greeting them, "I love you and I am here to help you." He said it got his heart and mind focusing on them, not on his own need for a sale.

That may sound a little strange at first, but isn't that the attitude we should be striving for? The only way that you can get what you want or need is to first of all help others satisfy their wants and needs.

A GOOD, FIRM HANDSHAKE

You definitely do not want to come across like Victor Vice or Fanny Fish. Your handshake should be firm, but adjusted for the person whose hand you're holding. Should you always shake hands? Not necessarily. Use your good judgment and knowledge of customs, particularly with people from other cultures. If you are unsure, don't shake unless your prospects move to do so. If you're meeting a woman who appears to be over sixty, and you are younger and male, let her make the first move.

It's quite acceptable now for a male to offer his hand when greeting a younger woman. In any case, the contact should not be too long, and above all, do not use both hands, placing the left hand on top. That can be perceived as patronizing and condescending.

A female agent should always offer a male prospect her hand and have an air of friendliness about her, but not too smiley or too friendly. She should present herself with professional warmth. This helps establish professionalism and authority in his eyes in case he is one of those "rare" male chauvinists.

What if you're greeting a couple and it's your call as to whom you greet first? If it is your call and they are side by side, then the safest thing to do is to greet your same gender first. It is even better to stand slightly to the side of that person. This helps to avoid even the slightest impression that you're being seductive with your prospect's partner. People can be really weird. Age has nothing to do with jealousy. You never know what these people have just experienced. They may have had a big spat about some flirting with the server at the restaurant. You just never can tell. Play it safe.

If you are an extrovert and you greet introverts with all of your natural gregarious skills, you can very easily drive them deeper into their shells. So, it's much better to come across a little softer, a little calmer, and a little less aggressive. This way you will not run the risk of turning anyone off. If you discover after a couple of minutes that your prospect is obviously quite extroverted, then you can let your extroverted personality shine.

Remember, you are already starting behind the eight ball because you're in sales. Don't make it any tougher by not being sensitive to the personalities of the people with whom you are dealing. After all, the aim of the greeting phase is for you to take control of the situation and you can't do that if you have somehow offended a prospective buyer.

In every sales situation, someone is always in control. It had better be you. You are the expert, the director, the leader. It is important from the very beginning to establish yourself as the leader, not in an arrogant, dictatorial way, but with a professional, take-charge type attitude. When you walk into a doctor's office doesn't the doctor take charge? Doesn't an attorney do the same?

Once the prospect indicates how you can help him (by asking for "a little information," a brochure, or perhaps to "see your model"), take charge with the use of mini-commands like "I'll be glad to help you with that. Just step over here, please."

Then turn and walk away. They will follow you 96.7 percent of the time. There will be times when the prospect is in a hurry or is more difficult to lead. You still need to continue to establish your control for the rest of the interview to go well.

This entire greeting and approach process may only last a minute or so, but it is so very important to do it in the right way. It must come across in a relaxed, caring way, not aggressive and not selling. You are now ready to lead them into the most important and yet most misunderstood part of the sales process: the initial interview and overview.

But first, let's take another look at what you're about to tell them. After all, there's no need to put your foot in your mouth.

CREATING A BUYING, NOT A SELLING, ATMOSPHERE

Remember the last time you went into a nice clothing store and heard, "May I help you?" Almost instinctively your response was "No, I'm just looking." We tend to resist any overt attempt to sell us something.

I hear many salespeople from all parts of the country presenting their credentials by saying, "I sold this unit to Dr. Jackson," or, "We sold twenty-five out of thirty of these lots."

They think they are doing something right by trying to persuade the prospect to realize how successful they've been, but in reality they are only building a barrier between themselves and the prospect. The prospect may start thinking, "Well, you may have sold all of them, but you're not going to sell me anything!"

We need to create a buying atmosphere, not a selling atmosphere. We must position ourselves as the facilitator, not the initiator of the transaction. Let the customer be the initiator. A much better way to convey activity is to say, "Dr. Jackson purchased (or bought, or selected, or chose) this particular homesite." Or, "Twenty-five of these thirty homesites were purchased within the first three weeks!"

Use language conducive to buying. Avoid prejudicial words. How often have you been told to never sign a contract without letting your lawyer see it? Why stir up mental anguish with your prospect by referring to it as a contract?

Why not call it something a lot less antagonistic like "paperwork," or a "purchase agreement," and then ask them to "approve" it?

I hear many salespeople talk about giving tours of their communities. If you see yourself as someone who gives tours, then you may be paid like a tour guide!

Instead, plant seeds of excitement in the prospect's mind by talking about going out and exploring your community, the mountain, or the island. Say, "Let's go out and discover what our community has to offer." Or simply, "Let's go out and take a look at our community together."

ABRAHAM LINCOLN, SALES ACE

We all need heroes in our lives. One of mine is Abraham Lincoln, who was a truly magnificent salesperson.

I realize that Honest Abe devoted his life to higher pursuits, and I, for one, am grateful that he did. However, if we study the man carefully, we learn that one of the secrets of his great success was that he was a master communicator and persuader of people. That's what a professional salesperson is. One of my favorite Lincoln quotes relates directly to sales:

When the conduct of men is designed to be influenced, persuasion, kind, un-assuming persuasion, should ever be adopted. It is an old and a true maxim, that a "drop of honey catches more flies than a gallon of gall." So with men. If you would win a man to your cause, first convince him that you are his sincere friend. Therein is a drop of honey that catches his heart, which, say what he will, is the great high road to his reason, and by which, when once gained, you will find but little trouble in convincing his judgment of the justice of your cause, if indeed that cause really be a just one.

Now, go back and read it again, slowly this time because this quote sums up the challenge of sales. If you can master what Lincoln is saying, you will become a master in the art of sales.

How do we influence people to take a course of action? By using "kind, unassuming persuasion." What does "unassuming" mean? It means "modest; not forward." In other words, listen to what the other person is saying. Develop empathy and understanding for his or her point of view.

43

"A drop of honey catches more flies than a gallon of gall." The honey of friendship is sweet. The gall of calculated manipulation is bitter. And in the end, a false show of friendliness — slickness, in other words — will only deceive a prospect.

What is the goal? To "win a man (or woman) to your cause," or in our case to a community concept and lifestyle that we believe in.

And how do you do it? By demonstrating that you are his or her "sincere friend." Frankly, the last way a prospect perceives us is as a sincere friend. They have preconceived opinions and ideas about us based upon past experiences with amateur salespeople who are the slick, fast-talking ones who are interested only in getting what they want.

When these prospects walk in surrounded by a wall of defensiveness the question is: How do we convince them that we want to be a friend? By doing just what Abraham Lincoln would have done. By treating each prospect with sincerity and understanding. By giving them honest, accurate information. Perhaps most of all by being a good listener. That's what I call being a true sales professional.

Brad Munday, who is consistently one of the top salespeople at beautiful Kiawah Island near Charleston, South Carolina, always makes this statement to prospects in his office within the first ten or fifteen minutes. While they are sitting around the table, he looks them in the eyes and says, "Could I just explain to you how I see our time best spent today? I'm not here to try and sell you anything you don't want to buy. But I am here to help you accomplish whatever it is you want to accomplish. Kiawah may or may not be right for you. It's not right for everyone. If I listen to you carefully and do my job right, though, who knows? It may be the right place and you and I may end up becoming friends and neighbors for years to come."

This is said from his heart with absolute sincerity. He says he often sees their posture relax, and that wall of defensiveness begins to melt. Why? Because he doesn't want to sell them? Of course not! He does if it is right for them. But he understands that the first step is convincing them that he is their "sincere friend."

Finally, Lincoln explains that when a person's heart is captured it is "the great high road to his reason." What does he mean? That people will justify logically in their minds anything they emotionally want to do in their hearts. In other words, people buy our product on emotion but must be able to justify that decision with logical reasoning.

Dale Carnegie stated, "You can make more friends in two months by becoming sincerely interested in other people than you can in two years by trying to get other people interested in you." How true!

Always remember that by their very nature people are self-centered. Your prospects will buy for one and only one reason: if they are convinced it is best for them and that it fills their needs.

And how are you going to find out what those needs and wants are?

I'll give you a hint: It has nothing to do with your mouth.

SOMEONE TO LOOK UP TO

All of us need other people to look up to, whether they are historical examples like Abe Lincoln or a role model/mentor who is currently alive. It helps to know others who have broken mental barriers, those who help to shake the shackles off of our own self-imposed limitations. I look up to John and Greg Rice. They are brothers and they are very successful businessmen.

And they are around three feet tall. They may be little in stature, but they are far from being small in mind or spirit.

Years ago they set up and ran a highly successful real estate practice in south Florida. They've been written up in numerous articles and featured on shows like *20/20* and are even in the *Guinness Book of World Records*. They worked strictly with high end clients, you know, "big" people. They drove a custom-built Cadillac while showing expensive homes.

At times, they had to ask to be put on top of the counter to demonstrate some of the kitchen's features. Did they feel the least bit intimidated? Not on your life!

I spoke with John at a National Speakers Association convention and asked him, "What has been most important in your real estate success?"

He looked at me and said, "I found something I love to do and became the very best at it. Since I love to do it, it's not like work." Simple, but oh, so true.

I asked him how he overcame what most would see as a big handicap?

He answered, "You mean my size? I've never even seen my size as a handicap."

Amazing! We tend to see whatever we look for, don't we? They looked for and found what they could do, not what they couldn't do.

John and Greg are excellent professional speakers. I saw John wielding a cane at the convention. I asked him what it was for. John explained that he had been in a serious car accident and had broken his neck in a couple of places. He had spent eleven months and ten days in the hospital in a complete body cast and had survived two operations. They took a piece of bone from his hip and fused the bones from the base of his skull to the fifth vertebrae.

He said, "I can't turn my neck, but I can still work my mouth!" What an inspiration!

A few months after the cast was removed, he decided that he would attempt to make his first speech. He said that he wanted to see if he could still travel. He looked at me and said, "I felt that if I could negotiate the Atlanta airport I could handle about any place in the world!"

The next week I was going through the Atlanta airport. Even though I had been there hundreds of times, this time I saw it in a different light. I was carrying a suitcase, a briefcase, and some boxes. I was walking among huge crowds of people who were scurrying down the concourse and the escalator to get to the next concourse to claim baggage.

As I observed this sea of people, I wondered what if I had to use a cane and had a stiff neck with a back that was in constant pain? What if I was only about as tall as the handrails that I was holding onto? How would I make my way among all these giants? Well, it didn't stop John. In fact, just the thought of him caused me to stand a little straighter and walk a little taller. The boxes and luggage I was carrying didn't seem as cumbersome as they had before.

John may be little, but he certainly isn't small. Not in his thoughts, not in his actions, and not in his life! John Rice passed away in November, 2005. I believe he is in a much better world. He accomplished a great deal while in this one. John may have been little in stature but he certainly was not small. Not in his thoughts, not in his actions, and certainly not in his life! No doubt a small part of his mission was to touch my life –

Even during a brief interlude….He made me believe BIGGER!

What excuses do we tend to make for what we think we can't do? Why shouldn't we reprogram our thinking to start finding ways to do what we want to do like John and Greg Rice, a couple of giants I have looked up to for years?

LISTEN UP

How often have you heard someone say, "Old Joe could sure make a great salesman because he's certainly got the gift of...listening"? Probably never.

Yet observant and attentive listening has as much to do with your success in sales as do your verbal skills. Probably more.

How important do you think attentive listening is to a physician for making an accurate diagnosis? How important is observant listening to a detective in solving a crime? Or to a lawyer in obtaining a verdict? It's the same in sales.

Every person you sit in front of has situations in his or her life that need to be addressed. They all have problems that need to be solved. They all have needs and wants. One of the most important parts of this game is for you to learn and understand what they are.

Buying real estate, whether it is a primary home, homesite, or a second home is an activity charged with emotion. For the majority of people, buying real estate is the biggest financial decision in their lives. Before they take that step, they need something more than a good intellectual argument that this is the right decision for them to make. It's got to *feel* right!

- They must feel that your community and property serves their needs and fulfills their wants.
- They must feel that they'll be proud of owning it and showing it to their friends.
- They must feel a strong degree of confidence in the stability and integrity of the developer and builder.
- They must feel that they are getting a good value for their money, that they are getting more than they are paying for.
- They must feel that they will have good resale potential in the future and that their financial investment will be well protected.
- They must feel that the general location is right for them.
- They must feel that they can trust you.
- They must feel that they like you as a person.

The question is: How do you get a prospective buyer to feel like this? First of all, you must have those feelings yourself! If you have a sense of integrity, and I assume that you do, it's hard to sell something that you don't believe in, including yourself.

LOOKING GLASS SYNDROME

Many salespeople suffer from a condition I call the Looking Glass Syndrome. Psychological studies show that the average person spends up to 90 percent of his day thinking about himself or something that directly affects him. When he peers into that looking glass, he only sees one thing: himself.

One vital key to success in our business is consciously making the effort to put that particular piece of glass down and pick up another type of glass, a magnifying glass. Look through this magnifying glass as you spend time with these people. It will magnify their needs, their wants, their dreams, and their ambitions. Seeing these clearly helps you to help them. As the great speaker and motivator Zig Ziglar once said, "You can have anything you want in life if you just help enough other people get what they want." This is the perfect philosophy for our business!

The following is a good way to start your day while staring into that looking glass. I did it practically every morning while selling books:

This is the beginning of a new day. God has given me this day to use as I will. I can waste it or use it for good, but what I do today is important because I am exchanging a day of my life for it. When tomorrow comes, this day will be gone forever, leaving behind — in its place — something that I have traded for it. I want it to be gain and not loss, good and not evil, success and not failure, in order that I shall not regret the price that I have paid for it.
— Samuel F. Pugh

$$4$$

THE INITIAL INTERVIEW AND OVERVIEW

Do prospects come to you because they are interested in your community? Not necessarily. Usually they are only curious and to assume any more than that would be erroneous. The last step in marketing before you take the baton and run with it is the cultivation of curiosity. When this curiosity creates enough pressure inside the prospects, they will either call or write for information or drop by your sales office. They may be there to see your community with the same goal in mind that they had when they visited other communities, with an **attitude of elimination.**

The goal of the initial interview in the office is to convert them to having an **attitude of anticipation** before seeing your property.

We must casually, confidently, and cautiously collect information about their likes, dislikes, activities, background, and dreams. Then we know where and how to aim our arsenal of information to ignite their interest and gradually convert their curiosity into genuine interest. I say cautiously because this information must be gathered indirectly in a conversational manner, not through interrogation.

Gathering information in the right way helps us to better position ourselves to present our features and benefits. Our prospects' interest thermometer level must be raised before they are ready to see, much less to buy, anything. And the only way for you to know how to accomplish this is by listening carefully and sensitively to what they have to say about their hopes, dreams, and fears.

THE INITIAL INTERVIEW, PHASE ONE

Okay, the prospective buyers are in the office waiting somewhat nervously for something to happen. It's up to you. What do you do?

I've found that one of the challenges many sales execs have is leading the prospects where they want them to go. A good way to handle this follows. These are called "transitional statements" and are used to move them from the greeting area to the regional maps, then to the sitting area (round table, couch/chairs, etc.) in order to get into the interview/overview specifics.

After a little chitchat at the greeting such as where they are from, first time here, how they heard about you, etc., you move on.

Transition: "Well, Jason and Ashley, what folks like about the way we do things here at ___, in order to save you time, I'll go over some high points and answer some questions. If you find us interesting we'll open up the site map and get into more specifics. How's that sound?" (This is general and easy to commit to.)

Immediately following the transition statement say, "If you'll step right over here, I'll be glad to help you." And then with an air of assumption (I use this word because leadership is assumed, not assigned), turn and lead them to the regional location map.

Proceeding from there, try asking them some of the following questions:

- "Jason, I see that you and Ashley are from Chicago. How long have you lived there?"
- "How do you like it?"
- "How often do you get down this way?"
- "Are you planning a move to our area, or are you just visiting?"
- "How do you happen to be out looking at homes today?"
- "How did you happen to hear about us?" (If you already know, dig deeper.)

You need to respond to their answers to these questions with reflective comments in order to keep this first meeting a conversation and not an interrogation.

And then, still very conversationally, begin to tell the new prospects about the community you represent. For example, "Why don't I give you a brief overview of Wellesley and why so many people have been excited about us? If you like what you hear, then we can spend as much time learning about Wellesley as you like. By the way, what attracted you to this part of the country?"

Then present three or four attention-grabbing points about your community, such as why so many people are attracted to it and the number of purchasers during the last year. You need to be sure and weave in some general price ranges of your properties in order to determine if the prospects are comfortable with that. It will save you time and save them possible embarrassment.

Say, "If you find Wellesley appealing, you're here at an excellent time, because …" And then give a couple of good reasons why the timing is excellent to purchase now.

Then test the waters to find out their reaction to what they have heard:

You: "How is it sounding so far?"

Prospects: "Pretty good!"

You: "Would you like to learn more about us?"

Prospects: "Yes."

Transition to table/site map: "Great! Let's step over here. We'll discuss what you're trying to accomplish and I'll give you an overview of ____. If we find there's a possible match, we'll jump in the car, take a look at the models and learn as much about ____ as you'd like. Can I get you a cold (or hot) drink before we sit down? "

At this point, step over to the receptionist and say in a voice loud enough for the prospects to hear, "Please hold all my calls. I'll be with Mr. and Mrs. Jones for the next thirty minutes or so."

This simple phrase accomplishes four things:

1.   It makes them feel important because you're giving them your undivided attention.
2.   It suddenly positions you as being even more in control.
3.   It avoids annoying interruptions.
4.   It lets the folks know that you're planning on being with them for at least thirty minutes so they can relax. If there's a problem with that, it will come up then and can be handled.

Then direct them to one of the following: your office (if it is large enough to be comfortable and looks reasonably neat), the conference room, a table on the deck, or a conversation pit set up in your sales office area.

At this point you are ready to begin the second phase of the initial interview.

THE INITIAL INTERVIEW, PHASE TWO

Just relax with them a few minutes getting to know them a little better. Then explain the three primary keys to successful real estate ventures, especially when dealing with planned residential communities. Your prospects probably expect you to say, "Location! Location! Location!"

The three keys really are: *location, timing,* and *concept.*

Think of them as the legs on a three-legged stool. Which of the three legs is most important? All of them are of equal value, aren't they? If the location is great but the prospective purchaser is not convinced that it's a good time to buy, then the transaction will probably fail. Or if the location and timing are fine, but the concept of the community is not appealing, then it will also have problems. And so on. All three must be acceptable in order for the venture to be successful.

You probably noticed that in the opening phase of the initial interview, we focused primarily on location and timing. In this phase, you will be able to concentrate on the concept of the community itself, or what makes it uniquely desirable.

However, the first thing to do for your prospective buyers, who by now are seated in your office or conference room, is to offer them a beverage of their choice. This little ceremony is not only a way for you to show the prospective buyers that you intend to be their friend, but it also slows things down which is exactly what you want.

Be sure that whatever they drink is served in a nice mug or glass. No paper cups, please. You want to demonstrate that you represent quality.

If you have a video of your community, now is a good time to let them see it. "Jason, Ashley, to give you the best understanding of our community in the shortest amount of time, let's go into our video room for about five minutes or so and watch a movie that hits all of our high points. Then we can sit down and chat for a while about your impressions."

As you sit down, be relaxed and cordial. Ask about their feelings regarding the video. Listen carefully for any common ground, and then share information about yourself. Those big steel bridges that we sometimes cross are not built from one side all the way to the other. They are usually built from both sides to meet in the middle. Bridging a relationship with a prospect is the same. It needs to be a two-way street. They must feel that they are getting to know you not only as a salesperson, but also as a person.

We are trying to create a buying atmosphere, not a selling atmosphere. Emphasize the good fortune of their timing because unless value and urgency are established, a decision will not be made.

As you unfold the site map with pen in hand, you can start explaining the concept and vision of your community like what makes it unique, desirable, and valuable to so many other owners. This needs to be well-organized and planned. You don't want to turn this into a fifteen-minute presentation, though, so it also needs to be conversational.

I don't know anyone who's better at this than Johnny Ussery, a top sales ace at Berkeley Hall just off Hilton Head Island, South Carolina. Here's how he does it.

He says, "One thing people seem to appreciate about us here at Berkeley Hall is that we are so low-key and laid-back that it's ridiculous. So, you certainly won't get any pressure from me. The one thing I will do, though, is explain the concept of our community, and once you see it and fully understand it, then if you are like most everyone else I work with, you will have one of two reactions. You'll either say, 'This is just great. We love it. It feels right to us and we want to become involved with it.' Or, you'll say 'It's nice, it's beautiful, it's probably fine for some people but it's just not the right place for us.'

"I want you to feel totally comfortable telling me either one of those things. At any rate, as you begin to learn more about us, if it is the kind of concept you'd really enjoy being a part of, your timing couldn't be better."

Then you continue with:

"We talked about location and timing. Do you remember that last vitally important key to a successful community? Concept. Our movie hit the high points, but as I give you a broader overview of our concept here, be thinking about whether it's enough of what appeals to you to warrant taking a closer look at the property. Okay?"

After a few minutes of this warm-up chat in which you have begun to establish some rapport, don't be afraid to take some good notes. Actually, this will impress them that you are listening and care enough to jot some things down. In fact, explain exactly what you are doing.

Say, "Let me just jot some of these things down. I have a good memory; it's just that it's too short sometimes." Or, "I've always heard that a short pencil is better than a long memory, so let me just jot some of these things down so I won't forget them."

MOUNTAIN - VALLEY APPROACH

Keep in mind that these people are here to get information, not to be interrogated. We can't hit them with a lot of questions, one right after another like a machine gun. It's important to weave questions innocuously into your interview.

I call this the mountain-valley approach to interviewing prospects. The mountain peaks are the features and benefits that you wish to point out to the prospective purchasers. The valleys are where you ask the questions to get the information about them that you'll need to properly shape your sales strategy.

By going from the mountaintop to the valley and back again during your conversation, you create a give-and-take atmosphere that puts the prospects at ease and lets them know you care about their needs and wishes.

Most salespeople know all about their product and are anxious to share this knowledge. They feel more confident telling what they know rather than listening to learn what they need to know. They do not realize that the best way to become interesting to a prospect is to be interested in the prospect.

Keep in mind the old saying: "People don't care how much you *know* until they know how much you *care.*" After all, this information you're gathering is to be used later to customize your presentation to them. If you're giving the same presentation to everyone who walks in, that is like having a shoe store with only one size and one style.

In the course of the initial interview, you will want to share with prospective buyers:

- features and benefits of the community
- stories about other owners and why they purchased
- a developer or builder story to establish confidence in the financial stability
- amenities offered and enjoyed by owners
- values of properties (ones already purchased, ones for sale).

At the same time, you will gather information from them about such things as:

- any plans for their current home
- moving to this area or is this a second home

- family information, i.e., children, grandchildren, in or out of the house and where they live
- family members nearby
- any friends who have purchased in your community or area
- types of activities enjoyed
- property being considered: permanent, vacation, retirement, second home, rental
- amount of time they have been looking
- other areas they may have been considering
- what other communities they've actually visited
- favorite one so far, and why
- reason for not selecting it, or what it lacked that they are still looking for
- the optimal timing for their purchase
- financial parameters
- type of house or condominium they hope to buy or build.

So, as you're shouting from the mountaintops the advantages of your community, you must dig answers from the valleys in order to learn a lot more about the people who have walked into your office. The more you know, the easier it will be to customize your presentation.

As you are "shouting your benefits from the mountaintops," do not do so like a waiter reading a menu. Speak from experience. Describe the amenities as activities that people are enjoying. Describe people involved in some concept of living within the community.

Successful developer Jim Chaffin said, "People who are buying into these types of communities are more concerned about life experiences than simply lifestyle. Their well-being is more important to them than just being well-off."

There will be times when you are with a couple and there are no other people around the office. The prospects may be wondering if they are the only ones to have discovered this place. You must then verbally create an aura of activity by describing (using the map or topography table) buyers who came in, what they bought, and why they bought it.

Prospects must sense that things are happening! They want to be a part of something that is successful, so you must create that success verbally if they can't see the activity taking place visually.

TAKE YOUR TIME

Overall, there are eight things you must accomplish during the course of the initial interview.

1. ***Establish rapport.*** Your clients must like you and begin seeing you as a human being who cares about their interests, not just a salesperson only interested in yourself and trying to sell them something. This is the foundation.

2. ***Be sure prospects understand the "life concept" of your community*** – why it was created, the purpose it serves, the type of people who are attracted to it.

3. ***Establish the integrity and financial stability of the developer or builder.*** It would be good to have pictures on the wall of the builder, family members, and the entire development team. Background information (awards won, etc.) needed to establish credibility should be on display. Humanize the builder or developer. Create belief (if it is true) that this developer is the type who under-promises and over-delivers. If there is little or no debt on the property then that also needs to be emphasized. It helps because this enables the prospects to understand that their hard-earned money will be protected.

4. ***Establish value in the mind of the prospect.*** Give prices of properties purchased, description of various amenities, quality of construction, clubhouse, location, shopping availability, schools, parks, lakes.

5. ***Establish financial ability to qualify.*** Make sure you're spending your time with genuine prospects.

6. ***Entice prospective buyers*** with stories and third-party testimonials from owners.

7. ***Create an aura of activity*** with stories of others who came in with no intention of buying, but found what fit them. They are now happy, active owners. This needs to be done verbally but can also be done visually using a community directory of current owners or a welcome board with names of your newest owners or members.

   If sales have been quite strong, then it may be of great value to have a six-month running list of owners showing who purchased in each month. This could include their first initial and last name, hometown, state, the property purchased, and price. The list should be updated each month, adding the month just ended and dropping the oldest information of the six months shown. Create that sense of success, the bandwagon that everyone wants to hop on and ride.

8. ***Narrow down the areas.*** If your community is quite large, or if you sell in multiple communities, then through the use of well-thought-out questions, various areas will need to be eliminated. You must start narrowing down the areas of the community, the price ranges, and types of properties you are going to focus on. One of the biggest mistakes made by salespeople is showing too much and confusing the prospect. Remember: a confused prospect never buys.

All eight of these steps need to work together to accomplish the primary objective for the initial interview. The objective is to move the prospect emotionally from being curious to being interested.

Two mistakes are commonly made in this important part of the sale. The first is that it is given too little time. A little rapport is built, a little information is given, and then the prospects are ushered into a car and toured around. The second mistake is to give it too much time, so that the prospects get bored, or they feel like they have enough information and don't need to look at the property. Good judgment and a good balance must be maintained.

A proper foundation is necessary for building a good house and a proper diagnosis is needed for accurately prescribing medical treatment. Likewise a good, thorough interview of your prospect as well as a proper overview of your community is absolutely essential for you to maximize your sales.

Now the question is: How do you become a master question-asker?

The only thing certain about the future is that the future is very uncertain.
— T. L. Weaver

5

MASTERING A NEARLY LOST ART-- QUESTIONING AND LISTENING

The art of asking questions is the key you need to open your prospects' minds and peer into the depths of their lives. Once you have learned how to use this art, you are well on your way to becoming a sales ace.

It's not only important to use the right types of questions, it's important to ask them at the right times. In the initial interview in your office the vast majority of questions should be open-ended questions. You are trying to open up the process and get the conversations flowing. Open-ended questions require greater expression than yes or no answers. Open-ended questions never start with these words: do, did, have, are, could, would, should, can, or will.

Rudyard Kipling wrote:

I had six honest serving men.
They taught me all I knew.
Their names were where, what, and when,
Why, and how, and who.

Your questions at this point should start with Kipling's "honest serving men," his w*here, what, when, why, how,* and *who,* but also add *which.*

A twin to the open-ended question is the open command. It accomplishes the same thing, but in a different way. It also adds to your flexibility so that you won't sound like you're stuck on just a couple of questions. The "open command" questions begin with phrases such as:

- "Tell me..."
- "Talk to me about..."
- "Describe for me..."
- "Explain what you..."
- "Give me your ideas on..."
- "Help me understand..."

Most salespeople make a serious mistake by taking the prospect's answers at face value. The information upon which they determine the future direction in which to lead their prospect is often based on superficial answers. How many times has a naive salesperson heard, "Oh, we're only looking today. We're not here to buy anything," and took that answer as fact? Consequently, the prospect was treated as if he was "only looking" and possibly a good buyer was lost.

That's about as silly as the old prospector walking along the hills and saying, "I don't see any gold lying around here." How absurd! He has to dig for it!

Same here. If you're going to get below the surface to those answers, which are like nuggets of gold, then you have to implement a very useful tool. In sales, it is sort of like your spade. In fact, in the late Frank Bettger's excellent book, *How I Raised Myself from Failure to Success in Selling*, he dedicates an entire chapter to it, and calls it "the most powerful word available in sales, but...one of the least used." What is the word?

The word is WHY. It's the perfect tool for digging below the surface if it is used properly.

And why do salespeople shy away from using this word? Maybe it's because they feel they are being confrontational. It can be if it is not properly applied. If you feel that you are coming across as confrontational by using the word "why," then try softening it with introductory phrases such as:

"Oh, really? Why do you feel that way," or "That's interesting. Why would that be so important to you," or "I've never thought of it quite that way. If I may ask, why do you say that?"

If "why" is used in a soft, sincere manner, it is quite powerful in retrieving the gold nugget answers that you want.

Keep in mind that you are striving to develop the skills to sell in a subtle way, not overtly and aggressively. It's like the difference between fly fishing and surf fishing. Surf fishing requires heavy tackle and makes a big splash and disturbance in the water when it hits.

Fly fishing is just the opposite. It is extremely light, and one of the many goals of the fly fisherman is to develop finesse in casting the fly into the water so that it is presented to the fish with a super-soft touch. The sales ace is like the master fly caster.

If you listen carefully and concentrate on what's being said, if you are observant and think, and if you word your questions properly, you can cast them into the stream of conversation without causing any disturbance or uneasiness in the prospect. Then you can reel in his or her attention, answers, and emotions.

In fly fishing, the fly is carefully cast just in front of where the trout is believed to be. It is then carried to him by the current, naturally posing a tempting delicacy. If you think about it and know where you want to lead your prospect's thought process, you can effectively do so by casting questions right in front of where you want the prospect's thoughts to be. In other words, **the one who asks the questions controls the direction of the conversation.**

For example: "With our one-thousand-acre lake, tell me how you would see your family enjoying it."

As a sales ace, you should also know when and how to use directional and tie-down questions.

Directional questions require a yes or no answer. They show you which direction to carry the conversation. Don't use these questions very much in the opening, or you will find yourself doing most of the talking and getting very little information. This type of question should be used more toward the close.

Directional questions can also be used for a summary close, as in:

- "Let's go back and review for just a minute if we can to make sure I'm understanding your feelings."
- "Did you feel you would get a lot of use out of the lake?"
- "Do you like the five miles of bike paths?"
- "Can you see yourselves using the club quite often for dinner, parties, and other activities for your family and friends?"

Tie-down questions are designed to confirm agreement with a statement. The tie-down question helps to strengthen the mutual understanding between you and your prospect. It should be used with a positive statement as a lead-in: "Why, it'd be pretty romantic for just the two of you to take that boat out on the lake, have a good glass of wine, and enjoy a beautiful sunset together, wouldn't it" or, "Having round-robin play at the tennis club helps in making new friends, doesn't it?"

There are numerous tie-downs you can use, such as:

- "Didn't it …?"
- "Haven't you …?"
- "Wouldn't you …?"
- "Couldn't you …?"

You can also create some good affirmative questions through the use of phrases like "Don't you agree?" or "Isn't that right?" Just be careful not to overuse this tool, or you come across as too blatant in your approach.

When leading a person to a desired outcome, move very slowly. Keep in mind that "persuasion by the inch is a cinch, but by the yard is hard."

As you head toward the end of your presentation, you may decide to review previous points of agreement so they can be refocused and elaborated upon. This is the reason for having good notes, or a very good memory.

The refocus question brings the prospect's mental state back to what we want them to be thinking about without telling them to do so in a dogmatic way. It helps to lock in their concentration on the positive and desirable parts of our presentation they are most attracted to. This type of question helps to gently and steadily lead the prospects to a desired conclusion. Here are some examples:

- "Tell me again, if you would, the kind of activities that were most appealing to you folks about the lake."
- "How important do you feel those memories would be to your children?"
- "How would you have liked having those kinds of memories with your folks when you were kids?"

Are you beginning to see how the answers to these questions might guide you in shaping your approach to a prospective client? Good. Now all you have to do is be prepared to really hear them, but that might not be as easy as you think.

THE ART OF ACTIVE LISTENING

A four-year-old boy picked up the phone and called his grandma. He said, "What are you doing, Grandma?"

"Oh, Grandpa and I are just talking," she said.

"Well, then," said the youngster, "who's listening?"

Good question. Who *is* listening?

Not enough salespeople are listening. Without a doubt, the most important, most crucial, most effective and yet the least-used skill in sales is the art of *active listening*.

Amateur salespeople who try to force sales usually attempt to talk a person into a buying decision, but the real pro, the ace persuader, has learned the art of negotiating a buying decision by "listening" people into it. The master salesperson accomplishes this through strategically placed questions and thoughtful, undivided attentiveness to the answers.

The questions we've just discussed are designed for specific purposes. Early in the initial interview, the open-ended questions yield a rich harvest of insightful answers that can give the master persuader several directions to take with his or her presentation.

Here's an example:

Sales Ace: "Since we've been talking about vacationing, what would you say some of your best vacation memories are?"

Prospect: "I remember when my dad, my grandparents, and I would go fishing on the pier and take long walks on the beach."

The ace salesperson would listen for and hear a lot more than the superficial answer. The master would hear and remember the heartbeat, the emotion of creating memories for the prospect's children or grandchildren, the need for a slower and simpler life.

Then at the proper time in the presentation, the ace would rekindle those emotions by creatively constructing a word picture while demonstrating a home or homesite near a lagoon, a lake, sitting on a mountain looking over the valleys, and closing that micro-sale with a properly positioned question.

If salespeople commit the mental energy necessary to truly listen, checkout the following benefits:

- A tremendous amount of time is saved.
- A more accurate assessment may be made of the direction the presentation should take.
- A more effective closing can happen.
- You feel less like you are pressuring people into buying.
- It makes the prospect more comfortable, as though he or she is in control.
- You will get more referrals because of the prospect's non-threatening experience.
- More sales are made; therefore, your income increases greatly.

All of these benefits and more will come about by practicing the art of listening deeply — listening for ideas, feelings, pauses, innuendoes, prejudices, fears, concerns, joys, desires — not just facts. Learn to listen to people's hearts, not just their minds and mouths. So many salespeople make the sad error of becoming the "Energizer" salesperson that just keep going and going and going...

I ran across a poem a number of years ago. I have no idea who wrote it, but it could be adopted by many salespeople as their credo:

I love its gentle gurgle.
I love its fluid flow.
I love to wind my mouth up
and listen to it go!

Society has a distorted perception of what creates success in sales. If you ask the typical person on the street what one of the most important characteristics for successful sales would be, most would say the gift of gab. In reality, becoming a master at the skill of selling means developing the art of listening.

THE SOUND OF SILENCE

The best conversationalists are the best listeners. Think about the people you most enjoy being around. Are they not the ones who listen attentively to you and make you feel special?

How do you feel when you are around a person who talks incessantly? Does it make you feel important? Does it make you feel like he or she has your best interests at heart? Or does it create irritation, disgust, and maybe even anger? These are hardly the reactions you want from your prospects!

Why is listening so tough for so many people? One of the reasons is that listening tends to go directly against human nature. Whether we like to admit it or not, we are quite self-centered.

In fact, psychologists have shown that as much as 90 percent of our thoughts in a day are centered on ourselves or something that directly affects us. Each word that comes out of our mouths screams "Notice me!"

Even as babies, when we wanted something we screamed about it. How often is a small child praised for the way he or she is listening? Never! Children are usually praised for learning how to talk, so they gravitate toward the area that brought about the praise. And we all crave praise.

At least half of our formal education is spent learning to communicate. We spend 100 percent of this time being taught in approximately these percentages: 40 percent to read, 35 percent to write, 25 percent to talk, and 0 to 1 percent to listen.

Usually the only instructions we get about listening are to "Be quiet" or "Pay attention and listen!" That's not a whole lot of specific instruction, is it?

Why don't we just listen? Because we often have mental obstructions and biased attitudes that keep us from actively listening. The mental problem is simply that our brain is so powerful. It can process information at an incredibly rapid pace.

The average person can hear and understand between 600 and 800 words per minute, but the typical person speaks between 125 to 150 words per minute. That means there's a lot more activity that takes place in the brain of a listener while a person is speaking at an average rate.

Another reason we don't listen is that we tend to resist silence or a lull in the conversation. Salespeople often hate silence. They think if they can fill up all that silent space with words, the prospect is more likely to buy. Actually, the opposite is true. Too many words just dilute the power of the presentation.

Sometimes we don't like or respect the person who is speaking. We may have a judgmental attitude, especially if they're saying something that goes directly against our values. This prideful and judgmental attitude can be quite detrimental to us.

We can learn from Emerson who said, "Every man I meet is in some way my superior, and in that I can learn from him."

Another common reason we don't listen is that we are too busy thinking about what we want to say next. Here again, we are encumbered by this self-centered rather than other-centered attitude.

One problem many of us have is that the speaker's words jog our memories and remind us of our own stories. They tell us about their fishing trip, and before we realize it, we're in the middle of telling about our fishing trip rather than demonstrating sincere interest in what they are saying.

Many of us tend to interrupt. When the speaker says something that stimulates a thought in our minds, it drops like a gumball from our brains onto the backs of our tongues. Then it rolls rapidly out of our mouths without any regard for what we are doing. That's a tough habit to break, but it is something we desperately need to work on.

Another common problem that so many of us have is our desire to finish sentences for someone else in order to eliminate awkward pauses. Those who are blessed with quick minds often let their thoughts shoot ahead of what the speaker is saying on the assumption that they know where the speaker is going. When the speaker pauses, we open our mouths and finish the sentence for him.

I call this "walking on their words." It's also known as "taking the words out of their mouths" which is extremely unsanitary and rude.

If we neglect using our physical muscles, they atrophy and become weak. Our listening muscles are much the same way. Just as it takes a conscious decision to put our physical muscles through strenuous workouts, we also have to make a conscious decision to exercise our listening muscles.

The first principle is *the difference between hearing and listening.*

Hearing is the physiological process that takes place when sound waves enter the ear and rattle the eardrum and those little inner ear bones, which causes a chemical reaction in the brain. It's truly a fascinating process, but it's not listening.

Listening is the psychological and emotional result of hearing. Men seem to have more problems with this than women.

A husband can be sitting in his chair with a newspaper or magazine in hand as his wife expresses an opinion or thought about the events of the day. She may receive an occasional grunt or nod in acknowledgment, until she finally gets upset and walks away.

He then asks, in an innocent tone, "What's the matter?"

The answer is always the same. "Nothing!"

"No, really," he says. "What's wrong?"

"You weren't listening to me!"

"Yes I was," he says. "You said…." And he tells her exactly what she said.

Her response is, "You may have heard what I said, but you weren't listening to me!"

Now what does she mean by this? She means that her husband was not being attentive to her. This is the best definition for attentiveness I've ever heard: *Showing the worth of individuals by giving undivided attention to their words and their emotions.*

What was missing for the wife in this situation was the emotional response from her husband. People give attention to what is important to them, and usually their eyes reveal that. If the husband's eye contact was missing in that conversation, he sent a nonverbal message, loud and clear, to his wife: "I don't know anybody in this magazine or newspaper or really care a whole lot about what is happening in it, but it's got to be more interesting to me than you, because that's where I'm focusing my attention."

Is that really what he thought? Is that the truth? It may or may not be, but it doesn't really matter. If that is what his wife perceives, then it is true for her. Remember, perception is reality to the one who perceives it.

So how do we put these listening muscles into a strict exercise regimen?

- First, resist any temptation to hog the conversation. In other words, learn to be silent and let the other person speak. (Isn't it ironic that the words *silent* and *listen* contain exactly the same letters?) God gave us two ears and one mouth. Maybe there's a lesson about percentage of use to be learned there!
- Don't prejudge the speaker too quickly. This takes discipline. Don't overreact to the tone of voice or appearance. Try to listen to what is being said and the feelings behind those words.
- Develop a proper listening attitude. In other words, have a sincere interest in the other person with a heartfelt desire to help satisfy his or her needs. After all, that's the only way you'll get your needs and desires satisfied.
- Be consciously attentive to the person's words and feelings.

- Don't just assume that you understand what the person is saying. If there is any doubt, clarify what is being said with a question, such as:

"Let me make sure I understand what you are saying."

"Do I understand you to be saying …?"

"Correct me if I'm wrong, but I hear you saying …"

True listening is *active,* not *passive.* Just as a football receiver must stretch to catch that pass at times, so must we as listeners, stretch in order to catch what the speaker is trying to communicate.

Here's a tough one for many of us: Discipline yourself to not interrupt when the other person is speaking; don't walk on their words. Let them finish their own sentences and thoughts.

BODY LANGUAGE

Studies have shown that our nonverbal methods of communication send out far more messages than do our verbal skills. If that's the case, then we've got to make sure that our nonverbal medium, or our bodies, are sending out the proper listening messages.

Eyes. We've all been taught that whenever we speak to someone we should look them in the eyes. But that's not necessarily so. If a person has a strong personality and looks the person deeply and continuously in the eyes when he is speaking, this eye contact can become overpowering and can create uneasiness and discomfort in the listener. When we are speaking to someone, we should look them in the eyes when we are relating a certain point, glance away occasionally, then come back to their eyes to make another point.

On the other hand, when we are listening to a person, the most important thing we can do (besides keeping our mouths shut) is keeping our eyes open and locked on the eyes of the speaker. We've been taught that the eyes are the window of the soul, but the eyes also send out very strong messages to the speaker that "you are important and I am giving you my full attention." The deep and constant eye contact will help you be perceived as an attentive listener.

Remember, *we hear with our ears but we listen with our eyes.*

Head. Nod your head in a slow but unsteady pace. It should be used almost as punctuation of what you are hearing. This nodding sends back to the speaker a message of empathy like, "I am with you," or, "I understand what you are saying." The nod should not be steady or it will send out a boredom message (and look like a ceramic dog in the back of a '57 Chevy).

Head Position. If you want to see a truly good listener, watch your dog. When you are talking to him, he is looking you right in the eye and his ears are perked up. Notice the position of his head. Is it tilted about 20 degrees to one side? Now, he probably only recognizes his name, but it sure gives the appearance that he's listening, doesn't it?

We should do the same. You may have trouble perking up your ears, but you can tilt your head. Be sure though, to tilt it in the same direction as the speaker's head like a reflection in the mirror. That way, the eyes make two even parallel connections, almost like railroad tracks. This creates a much more open, receptive impression for the speaker.

Hands and Arms. It's always better to keep your hands where they can be seen. If you're standing, let them hang by your side instead of hiding or fidgeting with them. If you're sitting, keep them on your lap or desktop. Folding your arms sends a closed, negative message to the speaker, so keep those arms unfolded.

Facial Expressions. The last thing a speaker wants to see is an expressionless face. It makes him feel like he is a guest speaker at the city morgue. Your face, your eyes and eyebrows, and the muscles used for frowning and smiling need to send back nonverbal messages that reflect the emotion of a message that is being heard. If the speaker is telling you something exciting, then your eyebrows should go up. If the speaker is speaking about something serious, a slight frown or look of concern should be the response. No faking! You need to be listening for the emotion of the message, not just the words.

Vocal Responses. An occasional vocal response is quite helpful from the listener as well. Words such as "Uh-huh," or "I see," or "Really," let the speaker know that you are tracking his thoughts.

Posture. Whether you are sitting or standing, your posture should be comfortably erect. Attentiveness is demonstrated by slightly leaning our shoulders and head in toward the speaker.

Feet and Hands. Some people have a fidgeting habit. They have trouble sitting still. Tapping your fingers on the table, fidgeting with a pen, or shaking a crossed leg sends the message to the speaker that we are in a hurry and we are losing patience. So, take a deep breath, relax, and place your total attention on the speaker.

PRACTICE!

I realize that there is a lot of detail here. Incorporating all of these nonverbal listening techniques will be quite challenging, especially if listening has never been one of your strong suits. Let me encourage you to take one exercise at a time. Consciously focus on doing just one with every speaker that you listen to. Then do it until it becomes second nature. A good place to practice is at home with those all-important family members.

For most of us, listening is much tougher work than talking. That's why we need to work harder at it. It is the one skill that, if improved, could dramatically affect your success.

The great baseball player Ty Cobb said, "The thing that drives me crazy is ball players who won't practice what they are not good at."

WHAT DO YOU KNOW?

We may have heard over and over again, "Well, what you don't know won't hurt you." But in this business, nothing could be further from the truth.

Like most people in this life, I learned this lesson (as well as just about every other lesson that has to be learned before becoming a sales ace) the old-fashioned way: I messed up a lot of times.

If you're listening carefully to what I'm telling you, maybe you won't have to end up in all the same pitfalls.

An old acquaintance of mine is one of the greatest salesmen I've ever known. His name is Spencer. He owns numerous businesses. He came from very modest beginnings and has become one of the wealthiest people in America. Many years ago, I asked Spencer how he had achieved so much at such a young age. He looked at me and said: "Terry, I've learned I'll never live long enough to make all the mistakes myself. And I figure any fool can learn from his own mistakes but a wise person will learn from the mistakes of others."

It's up to you. Are you going to be wise? Are you listening? Are you learning?

Treat everyone as if they are big shots because someday, some of them will be.
— T. L. Weaver

THE COMMUNITY DISCOVERY--
THE PRESENTATION

Like an actor getting his mind set before the curtain is raised, like an athlete preparing for the big game, you, too, need to get your mind set in the proper way before you meet your first prospect. In fact, before you even go into your office, it would be wise to take a ride through some of your community to remind yourself exactly what it is that you're selling. In other words, you need to "buy it every day before you try to sell it." Just pause and think about why it is so special.

I remember when I sold real estate in the early '80s at Sea Pines Plantation on Hilton Head Island. My office was in Harbour Town, and the view out my window had beautiful live oak trees, Spanish moss, and the Atlantic Intracoastal Waterway serving as the backdrop for graceful yachts navigating up and down. I rode to work each morning through a canopy of beautiful live oaks with lagoons on both sides, habitats for great blue herons, snowy egrets, and an occasional alligator. But day after day of that natural beauty began to cause it to dull. It became mundane.

It's not unlike the security guard who passes by the *Mona Lisa* a hundred times a day. He doesn't even see her. It's easy for that to happen to you, too, within your community. Be sure to guard against that.

Remember the initial interview? Our goal was to move the prospect emotionally from being simply curious to interested. Once you succeed in doing this, they are looking at your community with an attitude of anticipation. Now we're about to move them up emotionally to the next level, from *interest* to *desire*.

Over the years, I have been taught that human beings have two primary motivating factors for doing anything: the ***avoidance of pain*** and the ***attraction*** *of pleasure.* But how do we tap into these two supreme motivating factors with our prospects?

We must have a good understanding of their past or current pain, as well as their future vision of pleasure. This comes from being extremely observant and attentive to them. Try to gain an understanding of some of their stressors.

- Are they frustrated with the traffic where they currently live?
- Are they fearful for their safety due to the increase in crime around their area?
- Are they feeling stressed out because of their job responsibilities and just need a place to retreat?
- Are they going through the empty-nest syndrome and want to make sure they have a place that the kids want to come back and visit with the grandchildren?

Once you have some good clues like a good detective, then it's time to trigger an *activation of their imagination.* They must begin to imagine what life would be like as a part of your community.

How? You must pre-plan a good generic presentation of your community with specific modules that address their specific interests. Planned, not canned. You must be flexible and organized. With planning and organizing, you will be able to present your message in the best possible way and also avoid saying some things you maybe shouldn't.

Be enthusiastic. Enthusiasm is contagious. Keep in mind, though, that you must use the correct type of enthusiasm. Some salespeople are too outwardly enthusiastic, which puts the prospect on the defensive. It makes them feel like they're being sold (which is the last thing you want to accomplish). In fact, let the prospect's demonstration of enthusiasm be a good guideline and indication of your own level of enthusiasm. As they become more excited, let your enthusiasm grow and show.

The key is to relax, be sincere, be well organized, and have fun! After all, isn't buying real estate supposed to be fun?

A good friend of mine found out the value of having a carefully planned presentation as she was enthusiastically telling a gentleman prospect about the value and quality of their golf course. In the process, she also told him about the club and how they had golf tournaments between the different clubs. Mixing the quality of the course and the club play together, she said, "One of the things that people really like about our area here is that we have inter-course tournaments."

As soon as she realized what she had said, she stopped and immediately said, "I mean inter-club tournaments!"

The gentleman looked at her, chuckled, and said, "Sign me up!"

You've got to create enough excitement and anticipation about life in your community so that for the prospect finding the right property means finding a key to open the door of this wonderful experience.

Top sales ace Brad Munday said, "I always spend a lot of time selling Kiawah Island before ever showing property. It's much easier to sell it because buying into the area and our community concept doesn't really cost them anything."

ASK YOURSELF: "SO WHAT?"

Learn to think beyond the obvious list of features of your community (the championship golf course, the big lake, the great mountaintop views). Think deeper and write out the benefits of these features.

If your community has a beautiful lake, say to yourself, "So what?" Pointing out the lake is not enough. You need to add the benefit, the emotional reward, of having the lake nearby. If you recite the size of the lake, the height of the mountain, or whatever, then you are only giving them information that causes them to think.

But you must make them feel. *What is a fact in their mind must become a vision in their heart.* Learn to verbally bridge the logical features to the emotional benefits with the use of bridge words such as:

- Therefore…
- Which means…
- Consequently…
- As a result of this…
- The advantage to you is…
- So…

Example: "Jason and Ashley, our elevation at the top of the mountain is over four thousand feet, which means you will enjoy at least a nine-degree cooler temperature even on the hottest summer day!"

73

Don't just wing it. With the help of other members of your team, brainstorm all the features and benefits of your community. Put together a chart, such as this one:

COMMUNITY BENEFITS	
Specific Features	**Emotional Benefits**
Streetscape	Interesting variety, appeal to the eye, ease of access
Security	Peace of mind
School	Involvement with Community
Golf Course	Lower Stress, entertainment of friends
Lake	Serenity, recreation, FISH!
Types of Owners	Trust, safety, friends

Think of your presentation as a doughnut. The facts and features represent the hole: hollow, empty, representing no emotion. The benefit portion is the dough, a tasty mental picture you can sink your teeth into.

Take the hole, surround it with dough, and it makes a very sellable item. Take the facts and features, surround them with your benefits, and you will have a great, sellable product, especially if your doughnut dough contains a heaping portion of third-party testimonials. What's a third-party testimonial? Funny you should ask....

YOUR MOST POWERFUL SELLING TOOL

R ding through your community must be more than a "show and tell" exercise. You need to make frequent use of your most powerful tool of persuasion: *third-*

party testimonials and stories. Slow down and casually relate good third-party stories concerning what others have said about what you're selling.

Advertisers invest millions of dollars to do precisely the same thing. Why? Because it works! Madison Avenue has researched it extensively. If it works for them, it will work for us, too.

In fact, top sales ace Jim Wedgeworth, who has been number one in South Carolina for more than ten years, said, "The way I sell, which is relaxed and laid-back, I'd have to say that the use of the third-party testimonials is the most important part of the sales process that I do." He continues, "It's a very subtle way of selling. People don't feel like they're being sold. They're just listening to what everybody else likes about it."

Third-party testimonials are persuasive opinions from others that help to sell your product or incremental parts of it. They can be used in a variety of ways throughout the entire sales process to:

- Build credibility and trust in the initial interview
- Create "activity urgency," the sense that things are really happening around here.
- Build anticipation before actually seeing the community.
- Sell various amenities and benefits of owning.
- Answer, as appropriate, a prospect's questions throughout the presentation.
- Respond to an objection in the close.
- Train the prospect to remember your name. For example, "I was with a couple just yesterday, and after looking at the view from that seventeenth green, they looked at me and said, 'Terry'... "

The reason third-party testimonials are so effective is that most people care what other people think, but they don't necessarily care what you think. They know you are paid to like it. Also, people would rather hear a good story than endure a lecture, which is what many community presentations end up being. If a third-party testimonial is used in the right way, it will be told like a story.

Sales ace Mike McManus from Kiawah Island related a story he heard: "A gentleman from Atlanta who I was working with said, 'Mike, here's the reason that we want to own property at Kiawah. I was standing on the dock the other afternoon fishing in Bass Pond. To my left was my twelve-year-old son and to my right was my eighty-year-old father. As I was looking out across that beautiful lake, I could see great blue herons catching their dinner, like we were trying to do. The sun was going down over the Kiawah River. A cool breeze was coming across the lake. My son was reeling his line in, and my dad was straightening out a tangled line.

'The whole experience just made me stop and realize how fast life is moving. In no time at all, my dad would be gone. I would be stepping over to the right, taking his place; my son would be the one in the middle, looking over to his left at his twelve-year-old boy. I just want to have a place here to pass down to future generations so they can enjoy the same experience.'"

Do you think a prospect would be more likely to buy after Mike tells this story?

MORE POWER PERSUASION THROUGH THIRD PARTIES

I think we'll agree that a third-party story can tap into the heart and activate the emotions. Not all third-party stories have to do this, but it is a good idea to include some of them in your presentation. If the prospect is not moved emotionally, he or she probably won't be moved physically to buy, either.

So, where do you get testimonials like this?

Well, some salespeople make them up. But that shows shallowness, a lack of integrity, and a lack of listening skills. If you ask questions, if you are observant, and if you listen, you will find these stories in a variety of places, told by:

- prospects — Mike's story was from a prospect
- purchasers — a good excuse to call and start collecting testimonials
- generic experts — people from the media and consultants
- other salespeople.

Every sales meeting should consist of at least a ten-minute testimonial time for sharing the best testimonials with the entire group, especially if you are new and you might not have any. You have to use someone else's, which is perfectly all right. You can say, "One of our salespeople was working with a couple the other day, and he said...."

One of the most important things you can do is to be a good collector of testimonials. Going out on a presentation without any testimonials is like going into battle with no bullets.

Years ago I asked sales ace Jim Wedgeworth how many such stories he had that he could draw upon. He said, "Oh, at least three to four hundred." Some he uses every time to sell specific aspects of the community.

For example: "I was with a lady from New Jersey a while back and she asked if we could walk down to the beach. As we walked up on the dune, she said, 'Look at the people!' and I started apologizing to her, explaining that it's usually not this crowded but it was the Fourth of July, one of the busiest days of the year.

"She said, 'No, that's not what I mean. What I meant is where are all the people? Where I'm from in New Jersey, you have to park a mile away and get there by ten o'clock in the morning just so you can get towel space.' I saw probably a hundred people up and down the beach. Compared to what we were used to, I thought it was pretty crowded.

"That lady has made me a lot of money," said Jim.

Jim uses this story to sell the openness and lack of crowds on the Hilton Head beaches. But he doesn't have to say it. He lets others do it for him.

If you are not asking questions or using third-party stories, then you are probably telling a lot more than selling. Top sales ace Johnny Ussery of Berkeley Hall believes that he lives and dies by his third-party stories. In fact, his entire approach is to "create the urgency" — a combination of "thirst" for the benefits and "urgency" for why they should do it now, so they will not lose out.

No thirst = no urgency = no sale. It's as simple as that.

SELLING VALUE

Your presentation must create an aura of success. Point out purchasers and relate stories about how and why they chose your community. The prices of those properties should be mixed into the information as well.

In order to create value in the mind of your prospect, you must know what is valuable to them. As you begin to determine these points of value through good listening and observation skills, be sure and zero in on these components of your community. Slow the process down and sell each individual part. Talk about the golf course, the beach, the peaceful views across the lake, the boating, or whatever it is they care about.

This particular aspect of the sales process is so crucial that we need to slow down things a little bit here in order to make sure that everything is perfectly clear. What we are talking about here is presenting information to a prospective buyer in a way that makes it personally meaningful to him or her. It happens in three steps: *set up, demonstration* and *close.*

SET UP
You establish a need or a want; you create a problem in the prospect's mind. Or perhaps you remind the prospect of a problem that should be solved. Why create a problem? Because you have the solution.

DEMONSTRATION
You demonstrate how this problem has already been solved or taken care of in your community or at the house you're showing.

CLOSE
You close with a question that will receive an agreement or simply an acceptance with the use of a tie-down question, i.e., "Isn't it...?" or "Wouldn't it...?"

Suppose you want to point out that the developer of your property is financially stable. One way you could do this is by stating straight out that the company paid its bills and was bonded, and after providing a few facts and figures, leave it at that. That's how an amateur salesperson might go about it; however, it probably wouldn't have the desired effect because facts and figures don't have any emotional weight. They don't get through to the parts of the brain that control human motivation. The fact that a builder or developer is solvent is hardly compelling.

The fact that the developer is paid up with his bills fits neatly into only one step of our three-step presentation process, the demonstration phase. Now all you have to do is figure out what steps the other two steps should be.

The best way to do this is to figure out what the actual benefit is when the problem is indeed solved, then work your way backwards. For example, what benefit arises from having a developer with financial stability? Financial security. And, thinking backwards, if a developer goes bankrupt, what can happen to those who have bought home sites? They can lose their investments!

Once you've gone through this process, which should get easier each time you do it, the otherwise dry fact of the developer's solvency takes on an entirely different meaning. Here's how it looks:

Set up. "Have you ever been part of a community or heard of a developer promoting a variety of things he was going to do, but unfortunately he went broke before delivering on that promise?"

Demonstration. "Our developer has no debt on this property, and everything I tell you about future amenities such as another golf course is bonded to ensure its completion."

Close. "That would probably make you feel a little more comfortable about putting your hard-earned money into a place like this, wouldn't it?"

There's more than one way of pointing out the value of the property you're selling. Johnny Ussery likes to drop in a teaser by driving past a site he intends to show, hitting the brakes slightly, and saying, "Oh, by the way, be sure and remind me to show you that one. It's one of the best values we have."

And then he drives on.

These main selling steps (set up, demonstration and close) need to be thought out, planned, and practiced. These principles should be demonstrated, not just talked about or shown. Why do it this way, rather than racing through the entire presentation at once? Because it adds much more value in the mind of a prospect.

What do you see in figure 2? How about a nice piece of fresh Key lime pie? What would you expect to pay for a piece of pie like this in a first-class restaurant? Let's say four dollars.

Figure 2

Now look at the whole pie in figure 3. How much would that cost you at a bakery? Probably ten or twelve dollars.

Figure 3

As shown in figure 4, the whole pie provides eight pieces. Eight pieces times the individual price of four dollars per slice equals thirty-two dollars. That's a lot more than the ten dollars for the whole pie. Since your goal is to create as much value perception as possible, slow down and sell your community and the experiences it offers by the slice instead of offering the whole thing at one time.

Figure 4

INVOLVE, DON'T JUST TELL

A few years ago, I had a call from Gordon Hillock at Kiawah Island. He is a top sales ace. He said, "Terry, I feel like I have my office presentation down, but my community presentation from the car seems flat and sort of dead. What should I do?"

I told him that since I had never seen his presentation it was hard to identify the problem, but that because he had been a teacher for a number of years he may have reverted to the lecturing mode.

I told him to involve his prospects more. Ask more questions. Make his presentation more conversational, not presentational. I also told him to involve his best prospects in a more physical way and let them try it on for size. He asked me how, and I said, "I don't know. You're smart, and it's your island. Think about the things that you enjoy doing, and you'll figure out how to involve those prospects."

A couple of weeks later, I got a call from a very excited Gordon. "Guess what just happened! Yesterday I was with an East Indian surgeon from New York along with his family. I took them out and taught them how to cast a shrimp net. We caught a couple of pounds of shrimp. Then I took them back to their villa and showed them how to cook them. The doctor said he was so excited that the first thing the next morning he was going to go out and buy himself a shrimp net."

I was beginning to think that Gordon had started himself a new business of selling shrimp nets, so I asked him if that was all that happened. "No, I almost forgot to tell you. He bought a beautiful homesite as well, and gave me the names of six other New York surgeons who also wanted some beach property."

The doctor's wife wrote Gordon a letter and said that the highlight of their vacation was the video that she took of the kids. They were so excited, running around the dock and catching the shrimp. She called it priceless.

Sales ace Mike Parker used to sell at Governor's Club in Chapel Hill, North Carolina. He loves to fish. Mike was working with a professor at the University of North Carolina Medical School. Late in the afternoon he asked, "Doctor Bob, do you like to fish?"

"Yeah," he answered, "but I have not really had time for it the last ten years."

Mike looked at him and said, "Let's just see if they're biting."

Mike produced his fishing rod and his favorite lure that he always carries in the back of his Jeep. He made a couple of casts into his favorite lake by the golf course. Then, as he handed the rod to the doctor he said, "Now reel it in real slowly and jiggle the rod occasionally to see what happens."

Bam! The rod began to bend practically double as the doctor's eyes widened. He pulled in a three-pound bass. The first words out of the doctor's mouth were, "Are there any sites around here, Mike?"

And Mike replied, "Yes, right over there on that hill."

That hill is where Dr. Bob built his home. Mike always related that experience to all of his prospects. He concluded with: "At least once or twice a week now, I'll see Dr. Bob with his eight-year-old son out on that small boat fishing on that lake. They may or may not be catching any fish, but one thing is for sure, he's catching some lifetime memories with his boy. That's what this place is all about!"

Just as an expert fisherman like Mike knows that certain lures attract certain fish, you must understand the likes, interests and desires that attract certain prospects. Then you must focus on creatively luring them into the community, not just touring them around it.

"But I don't fish or do shrimp nets," you may say. All right, just be creative in thinking through your community's various benefits to use as lures to attract your buyers.

Sales ace Jeannine Hallenbeck sells in a beautiful high-end community called Cordillera near Vail, Colorado. She told me once that she had a couple from the Northeast walk in. "The man was very open, expressive, and just loved the area. His wife just sat there, not saying a word. Her lips were pressed tightly together. After a while, I just looked at her and said, 'I can tell you must not be quite as excited about this area as your husband, are you?'

"That question broke the dam and out flowed her fears. 'I'm certainly not,' she said. 'I just know he's going to buy here and make me leave the city I love. I'm going to miss my shopping, the plays, my friends, everything. In fact, I'm so nervous, my throat is beginning to close up on me and I can hardly breathe.'"

At this point, Jeannine backed off completely. "It doesn't sound to me like you folks are ready to do any looking or buying until you have discussed this more carefully. Without some compromising, one of you will be miserable."

Then she told them a third-party story of a couple from the New York City area in a similar situation. "They found a way where they could both win. They kept a beautiful apartment in the city as their primary residence, and then bought a place here to use two to four months out of the year. In fact, after being out here more in the summer, she found that she fell in love with hiking, nature, rafting, and all kinds of things she hadn't imagined that she would enjoy."

Jeannine continued, "I tell you what. I'm going to call the club and arrange a couple of box lunches. There is a picnic table right over here on this site with a breathtaking view across the lake. You two can take your lunch, stay out as long as you like, and relax while you discuss this exciting option. I'll be here all afternoon."

Around four o'clock that afternoon her prospects came back in. Jeannine said the lady was a different person. She was relaxed, smiling, and friendly. The first words out of her mouth were, "Is the site where we picnicked for sale?"

"Yes it is," said Jeannine.

And the lady said, "Great, we found our spot. That's the one we want!"

Jeannine combined creativity with sensitivity. Backing away and giving a non-presentation type of presentation was exactly the right thing to do. That's why you can't just learn a canned spiel and give out cookie-cutter comments. Instead, you must customize your creations so that they cut into the hearts of your prospects.

Otherwise, you are performing like a brain surgeon by using all the facts like a scalpel to cut into the brain, causing them to think. The true sales ace plays more the role of the heart surgeon by using stories, questions, silence, and experiences as lasers to delve deeply into the heart, releasing emotions and feelings.

People won't buy into the concept of your community until it feels right. All you have to figure out now is when that time has arrived.

GETTING A YES TO THE COMMUNITY CONCEPT

Time now for a quick review.

What was the purpose of the initial interview? To move the prospective buyers from being curious to being interested.

What is the purpose of the community discovery phase? To bring the prospects along from being merely interested in what you have to offer to actually wanting it.

So, you as an ace salesperson have to be ready to answer the following question: How do you know when the prospect is ready to move to the next level?

When I was a kid, I enjoyed making fudge with my mom. When the mixture began to boil, we tested it to see if the batter was done by letting a few drops of it fall into a cup of cool water. If the drops formed a soft ball, then it was time to take the fudge off the stove. Often, to make sure our timing was right, we would have to test the fudge three or four times. Even then we usually had to eat it with a spoon.

Selling real estate is a little bit like making fudge, especially at this stage of your presentation. You need to test your prospects to see if their level of interest is "sufficiently cooked" before moving on to the next step. You do this through the use of trial closing questions designed to confirm their interest and agreement.

Pause occasionally throughout the presentation and sprinkle in some good "temperature-testing" questions, such as:

- "How is it looking so far?"
- "Are we sounding better to you than you expected?"
- "What are your feelings about the lake, security, golf course, views, the beach?"
- "Do these owners sound like the kind of people who you'd like to get to know as friends?"
- "How do you feel about our location with respect to shopping, medical care, schools?"
- "Could you see yourselves getting a lot of use from our clubhouse?"

These questions should be sprinkled throughout your presentation, not rapidly fired as a prosecutor might do. As usual, your tone should be conversational, not interrogational.

At times, you may find yourself showing some specific pieces of property before completing your community presentation, but that should be the exception rather than the rule. It's much better to feed them one bite at a time.

Many salespeople move way too fast. Give your prospects time for their imagination to start activating, and for their emotions to start rising.

SUMMARY CLOSE

Conclude your community presentation at one of its most emotional points. It may be the deck of the clubhouse, the beach club, or the mountaintop overlooking a beautiful view. Slow down, relax, and give a summary of what they've seen and heard. Feel free to write your own summary, but here's an example that might get you started:

"Well, Jason and Ashley, there you have it. That's Eagle's Roost community. If you are looking for a place with first-class security that gives you real piece of mind, we've got it. If you're looking for all kinds of memory-building activities, from rounds of golf on a championship course, to sailing, fishing, or skiing on this beautiful lake, we've got it. If you're looking for a location that is near all the shopping that you would ever need, but yet removed so you can enjoy the peace and quiet of nature — we've got it. *My question to you is this: are those the kinds of things you're looking for?"*

You want to use a summary close such as this with prospects who express strong interest. Then pull out the site map and review various areas along with price ranges to determine which areas to focus on. Here's a good transitional phrase to use after receiving a positive response to your closing question: "Great! Let's just pull out the map and take a look at the various areas again to decide where to start looking."

If you are not sure about your prospect's interest level, then rather than a direct close using a closing question with your summary, simply summarize the benefits of your community and move to the map to explain where they will be going and what they will be doing next. Often, experiencing the benefits of specific properties will trigger that imagination and raise the interest level to where it needs to be.

*A secret to excelling, if you are in business,
is to first of all make sure the business is in you.*
— T. L. Weaver

HOW TO SELL A HOMESITE

You have completed your community presentation by selling the overall area, using the set up, demo, and close technique for special features and amenities. You have used numerous third-party testimonials and human interest stories, and you have established value by pointing out various properties and purchase prices. You have mixed in numerous trial close questions and have detected their interest level rising. You have completed your summary close. And, based upon what you've learned about their likes, interests, requirements, and price ranges, you have noted a couple of areas on the site map.

You are now ready to sell your new prospects a homesite. But how do you know which ones to show?

If you have fewer than two hundred pieces of property for sale, be familiar with all of the properties. But be intimately knowledgeable about your top twenty of each type. Know at least five in each price range. You should have walked them by yourself or with your sales team and written out descriptions of the specifics on each site. You should know the sites like the back of your hand.

Know the exact location, size, tree cover, proximity to various amenities, elevation, view, comparable prices, and neighbors. Knowledge breeds confidence, and the more knowledge you have about your specific sites, the more confidence you're going to have in demonstrating them. Put in your study time and stay current.

Before you go to the chosen properties, be sure you have your sales tools:

- site map
- full-sized plat maps
- a pad of paper and extra pens
- boots, preferably over-the-calf to guard against dampness, weeds, or snakes
- insect repellent
- a tape measure (at least one hundred feet long)
- an insulated bag with cold sodas and water as well as crackers and cookies for everyone, because if they are uncomfortable, hungry, or thirsty, they may lose interest.

As you arrive at a selected area, slow down, point out sites that have been purchased and their prices, and offer third-party testimonials. This helps to re-establish value. The third-party testimonials not only help present the advantages of purchasing, but let people know what their potential neighbors are like.

As you present any specific area, ask qualifying questions, such as:

- "How do you feel about this area?"
- "How do you like the style of homes in the area?"
- "Do you feel this would be close enough to the lake?"
- "Do these sound like the kinds of neighbors you'd like to get to know?"

SHOWING WHAT YOU'VE GOT

If you have been observant and know your inventory, you know where you are going to lead them. And you are equipped with site maps. But before you go, review properties and their attributes with the prospects.

Never be afraid to repeat yourself. People don't remember what you say, but they need to feel that they know where they are going and what they are doing. Otherwise, they get confused, and **a confused prospect never buys.**

Rarely show more than four properties the first time that you are together with the prospects.

Showing ALL You've Got. There are three reasons people want to see "everything you've got":

1. They are not sold on you. They don't really believe that you have their best interest at heart, or that they can trust you as their eyes to select what's best for them to see.
2. You haven't controlled the situation so that they know your professionalism and the way you do business.
3. You have forgotten what business you're in. You're not in show business; you're in the sales business. Most real estate people show and tell: show all they've got, and tell all they know. That's the reason so many people in this business are broke except in extremely strong markets.

Let's assume you are demonstrating four homesites. The worst thing to do is to go out and show four that all fill the bill for what these people want. Here's why not:

1. Value perception is vital. The value is not just the money, but the value based on all points that are valuable to the prospect. In addition, value perception is based on comparison of one item to another. This is true whether it is diamonds, cars, or homesites.
2. If you show all the properties that fill their requirements, there is a good chance that you will simply create confusion. (Always remember that a confused prospect never buys.)
3. By showing all the properties that fill the bill, you are destroying any fear of loss that could take place. They are likely to say, "Looks like plenty of these to choose from. We'll just think about it for a while and get back with you in a few months."

Your primary goal at this point is to reduce the number of properties under consideration as soon as possible to the one-of-a-kind property that is ideal for them. It is the only way you can generate the fear of loss in the prospect's mind. That fear creates a sense of urgency for them to act.

Never write out a list of all the properties you're going to show! I did that when I first started sales at Hilton Head thinking it would demonstrate how organized and knowledgeable I was. Actually, it just locked me into showing all those properties when I may have hit pay dirt on property number two.

Do not arrange your property showings according to their geographical proximity unless you find it absolutely necessary.

Show each property with an attitude of sincerity, but reveal a little more enthusiasm with the ones you have placed in the "greater value" position.

SHOWING HOMESITES IN THE RIGHT ORDER

Your order for showing the home sites should be determined by their total overall value, as follows:

- First — moderate or average, your qualifier home site.
- Second — better than the first, in terms of overall value,
- based on their desires.
- Third — below average.
- Fourth — BEST.

The first site should be selected by you to gauge their likes and dislikes. It should be one in the middle of the price range they are considering; it should not be one of your best, or one that fits all their specifications. Hearing their dislikes about this property is just as important as hearing what they like. What you hear may cause you to identify another property as ideal for them.

Don't assume anything. Re-orient them on the site map. Then spread out the plat map on the hood of your car. Arrange the map the same way that the site is positioned. Explain the dimensions and point out the corners. Orient them to the site's location with respect to the various amenities. Explain any special information regarding the site, such as easements, building elevation, unusual shapes. Then proceed to the area where the site shows to good advantage. Tell them the price.

Now it's time to use your legal pad. You must get them involved in this process. By this time, they should be seeing you as an assistant buyer, not as a salesperson.

Draw a line down the middle of your page. Through the use of probing questions, determine and write down in the YES column what the prospects like, and in the NO column what they don't like about this qualifying site.

Of course you won't talk to them about a "qualifying site." After all, they may love it and buy it! Use better wording like: "Jason, Ashley, could I get you to help me? Only you know what you like and don't like. How about giving me your idea of the ideal site? Tell me everything you like and dislike about this particular one."

Probe and layer your questions by saying such things as: "Really? Why is that important to you?" Or, "What makes you feel that way?" *Listen carefully for what prompts them to give the answers — not just the answers they give.*

As you create your list, you should flip through other sites in your mind like a rolodex. That's why it's so important for you to know your inventory so well. By the time the list is complete, you should have the ideal site for them in your mind.

Be careful not to let them paint a picture of a site that you cannot deliver for good perceived value. Otherwise, you are setting yourself up for failure. It's sort of like putting a drag on a fishing line to keep the fish from running freely and creating a backlash. You don't want any snags.

Attempt a subtle close with this first site. They need to get accustomed to being asked to buy. For example, "The purchase price for this site is ninety-five thousand dollars. How does that sound to you? Do you like it well enough to own it?" Say this in a lighthearted, relaxed way.

The second site. Even if you have the ideal site in mind after the qualifying site process, the last thing you want to do is to go directly to it. The ideal site needs to be set up to create the strongest perceived value in the minds of the prospects. So, the next site may have one less negative and one more positive characteristic. Go through the same type of procedure and, for your close, insert an elimination phrase to begin narrowing down to the right site.

Here's an example of such an elimination phrase: "If you were going to select one of these two that you've just seen, which one would you choose?"

If they select the second site, then ask, "Do you feel you like it enough to own it?"

Judge the next step based on the response you receive. If they are excited about it, you will want to take them to one more that simply magnifies the value and advantages of this number two site. If they are not that excited, then move to the next site that you feel is closer to filling their requirements.

The third site is usually below average.

Please note, however, that there are two very acceptable and effective ways to demonstrate the ideal site you have in mind.

One way is to demonstrate the ideal site third, and then show one other site that offers less value to them. After that fourth showing, go back to the ideal site, number three, and take a closer look.

The other way is to save the ideal site until last. After showing each site, use an elimination phrase to keep one site at the forefront of their minds. Try both ways, and decide which one you like the most.

The fourth site is the best site. You have learned the type of view they like, the price range, and their desire for amenities. You are ready to position this home site in its most favorable light and to create the most perceived value....

SHOWING THE IDEAL HOMESITE

By this time from all of the answers they've given, and from all the oohs and aahs you've heard, you have a good idea of what they really like and which homesite is the ideal one for them.

Unless this purchase is being made solely for investment, the prospect is not buying this just to own a piece of dirt. He hopes someday to have a home on it. Since most people have a hard time imagining what a home would look like if one is not there, try to find a home that is already built or is being built. If a home is under construction on a similar site, take them to it and show them how it is situated on the site and the view of the driveway entrance. Explain the reason you are doing this is so that they can better visualize a home on this next site you are about to show them.

Then proceed toward the ideal site. Continue to sell the area and the neighborhood. Establish value by pointing out recent purchases; explain the proximity of the site to various amenities. If the price of the site is something that can be used to establish more value, hold off on the price, but point out others that are priced higher or have been purchased for more. You can use your plat or site map for this.

Walk the site with your prospects and show all the corners; explain any special features about the site. Next, you must verbally build a home on the site, with their help. Use questions rather than making a lot of statements:

- "Let's just use our imaginations a little. Would you be building a one- or two-story home?"
- "How would you configure your home to capture the best part of this view?"
- "I wonder how we would be able to save as many of these trees as possible."
- "What type of driveway would you like, such as U-shaped, circular, or any other?"

You must get them involved! Let them hold the tape so you can show them the setbacks so they can see how much space is available in the building envelope.

Pay close attention to them. Watch them with each other. Listen carefully. Remember, you need to be playing the role of a detective. You're trying to seek out and detect buying clues. After detecting some interest in them for this particular site, state the price and begin your trial close questions:

- "Ashley, how do you feel about this location?"
- "Do you feel this site satisfies the tree coverage you want?"
- "Is the proximity to the clubhouse close enough for you?"
- "How do you feel about the view?"

If you are receiving all positive answers, then progress into the closing questions:

- "When would you want to begin construction?"
- "Have you picked out your architect and builder, or would you like some recommendations?"

If you are still receiving all positive answers, create a reason to leave them alone for a minute or so.

"Jason, Ashley, before you get too excited about this one, let me run back to the car and call to make sure it's still available. With this market, it could have been purchased during the last couple of hours." This provides them a little room to check out each other's feelings, or room to buy.

Return with the good news, then attempt to close on paper. Use your yellow pad again. Explain to them by saying, "Jason, Ashley, since you seem to really like what you're seeing here, let me show you how it looks on paper."

Step over to them and explain the purchasing details: price, down payment, interest rate, and an estimate of their payment. Circle that figure and ask, "Does this feel comfortable to you?"

They say, "Yes."

That's your cue to say, "Then let's go back and pull this one off the market before someone else does."

In fact, if you have followed the prescribed steps, the sale will frequently go just that smoothly. But you wouldn't want it to always be that easy, would you? It'd be boring! Everybody would be able to do it, and your commission would be drastically cut.

It's when you start receiving some objections that the real fun begins. That's when you'll have to pull out those secret weapons of sales success, the ones that the top aces use. That's also when you'll have to start drawing on the inner resources that make the difference between an amateur and a sales ace – between someone who will probably quit when things get a little bit difficult and someone who has the character to stick it out to the end. Someone like you, or you wouldn't be reading this book!

If you form the habit of cutting corners, you'll soon be just going in circles.
— T. L. Weaver

HOW TO SELL HOMES AND VILLAS

Just what, you ask, is the difference between a condominium and a villa? Well, as I told a prospect some years ago who asked me the same question when I was selling property on Hilton Head, "about seventy-five thousand dollars."

To be perfectly frank, a villa is just a fancy name for a condominium, but it sure sounds classier, doesn't it?

With your highly-developed skills of detection, not only have you discerned your prospect's need for a shelter rather than a home site, but you have determined the type of home or villa that might be right. An obvious advantage of selling shelter is that less imagination is needed when buying a structure because what they see is what they get.

You have been through your initial interview and completed the community presentation. You have learned the type of view they like, the general floor plan that would work for them, the kind of construction, the price range, the amenities they need, etc. You have also discovered through the use of probing questions and keen observation the type of home or villa that would be right for them. You may not know the exact one yet, but the qualifier property will help just like it did in demonstrating home sites. In fact, much of the same know-how is necessary to sell either "dirt" or "shelter."

SHOWING WHAT YOU'VE GOT

Try not to show more than four houses or villas. Sometimes you may have to show more, especially if this will be their permanent residence.

For goodness sakes, don't be like the Realtor I bumped into at Winn Dixie one day a few years ago. She was standing by the canned food section and looked like she had been beaten over the head with one of the cans.

I asked her what was the matter.

"I just finished showing some people thirty-two houses today!"

I almost passed out when I heard her say this, because she had been in one of my training sessions several months before. You can bet your life that's not the way she was taught!

"They'll never buy," I said.

"Oh," she said, "they liked me. And when they do buy, they'll buy from me."

I checked back a few weeks later just to see whether they had bought. She was quiet for a moment on the phone, and then said, "Well, something came up in their family up north, and they are not going to be able to buy down here."

Now, you may be thinking, "Wait a minute, Terry. I had one like that one time who bought!" So what?! Look at the odds. Prospects like that are not worth the time they devour or the energy they sap. Place a higher value on your time.

SHOWING SELECTED PROPERTIES

If you are demonstrating four homes, do not go out and show four that all satisfy the requirements your prospects have. Here's why:

- Value perception is essential. The value is based on all aspects of the property that are valuable to the prospect. Also, value perception is based on comparison of one item to another, whether it is pearls, cars, or homes.

- If all the properties you show fill their requirements, there is a good chance that you will simply create confusion. (And remember, a confused prospect never buys.)

- By showing all the properties that fit their requirements, you are neutralizing the fear of loss they might well have and that's what you're trying to build up. They may say to you, "There's an abundance to choose from. So, we'll just think about it for a while and get back with you in a few months."

Showing more only diffuses their value perception and confuses them. They lose any sense of urgency to buy that they may have had.

HOW TO SHOW THE HOMES

I remember when our home on Hilton Head was on the market. We had built the home and it had quite good curb appeal. It also had a very attractive front yard with beautiful oak trees. It was set well off the road and overlooked a lovely golf course. What I noticed, though, is that nearly every agent who showed our home simply pulled his or her car all the way in front of the garage. They would then immediately get out and walk right to the front door, ready to show our home.

It's much better to show homes using the following guidelines:

- Park in the best curb-appeal spot if the home shows well on the out-side. If it doesn't, get them inside!
- Step back in order to see the entire home from the road.
- Mention the quality of the surrounding homes, the neighbors, the streetscape.
- Discuss the landscaping, the automatic sprinkler system, the trees.

Use your questions to reveal information:

- "How much do you folks enjoy gardening or working in the yard?"
- "Does the landscaping appeal to you?"
- "As you can see, this home has a dormer type of roof. How do you feel about the lines of it?"
- "Do you like double-hung windows like these, or do you prefer a casement window style that rolls out?"
- "How do you like the driveway going along the side of the home to a side garage, versus crossing in front of the house?"

It would be wise to hold back on showing all the outside benefits, such as the fact that it's only a two-minute walk to the beach, that it has a dock or a pool, or that it's only a short stroll to the clubhouse. Save these to add more value later if you need to in order to help you overcome objections.

As you listen to their answers, record what they are saying on the YES and NO columns of your pad. Give each of them a small pad to record their own impressions and to help them keep all their information organized.

Be careful what you say. Do not prejudice them toward the home. I remember a fine agent named Christine telling me about a home that had been on the market for a while. She said the owners had a couple of dogs and that the house had been closed up for a couple of weeks prior to showing it. Rather than preparing them by warning them that the house was smelly, she said, "I just want to tell you before we walk in that these people love animals."

She said that the prospects walked in, stood in the foyer, smiled, and said, "Yep, smells just like home." They bought the home for the asking price.

If the owner happens to be there, introduce everybody but avoid lengthy conversations. Smile and say to the owner, "Where will you be in case I need to ask you a question?"

Jim Wedgeworth once told me: "They expect you to do a lot of talking inside the house, so I don't. I let them absorb what's there, and do a lot of my selling with testimonials in the car between showings."

Let them relax and explore the home, discovering the features that are most attractive to them. If it's a resale for security purposes you want to keep your eyes open especially in the bedroom areas, but don't hover. Give them room to experience the house and possibly move their emotions into that buying mode.

A possible introduction phrase is, "Folks, allow me to point out some key features about this home, and then I'll let you just relax and discover other areas that may appeal to you."

Remember, by now they should see you as the assistant buyer, not as a salesperson. Don't over-sell.

Keep in mind also that men may have more influence about the site selection, but women definitely have a lot more influence over the home that is selected.

If they don't like a certain property, ask why and record their reason on the list. Then move on unless it is one of your "ideal properties." Rather than being on the defensive and trying to defend particular points of the property they dislike, attempt to come up with a creative alternative that can solve the problem.

This is a thinking business, so plan your strategy.

FEATURES TO POINT OUT

The rooms that create the highest degree of emotional involvement are the kitchens and master bedroom suites (or possibly the bath and the sitting area or study).

It is best to build momentum when showing a home by starting out with rooms such as the family room, living room, study. Place the kitchen near the middle to accelerate the interest level. The master suite should be placed near the end.

There are certain features you should point out in any home:

- quality of flooring: carpeting, hardwood, tile
- ceiling height, crown molding
- windows: style, manufacturer, double/triple pane, insulation potential, light, brightness in the rooms
- general room layout and advantages such as the master bedroom being on one side and the other bedrooms on the other to provide maximum privacy
- views and the peaceful experience they provide
- storage areas, attics, garages
- the number and type of heating systems, hot water heaters
- quality of appliances, if that is a positive feature
- size of the different rooms
- what does (or does not) come with the home
- when showing new homes, what is included, not standard; and what are optional features or custom, not upgrades.

If there are bonus rooms above the garage or in the basement and are not easily seen, save these for later to build more value if you need to. It's always a good idea not to fire all your bullets at once, but save a few for later.

Through the numerous questions you'll be asking, you should have learned what they like and dislike about their current home, especially the kitchen and master bedroom area. This knowledge should give you a good foundation for building discontent with their current situation. That is your primary goal.

As the late sales guru Dave Stone once told me, "Anyone who does not become discontented will simply leave, go back and sit on their assets and do nothing."

There is also a standard list of questions you need to ask while demonstrating the kitchen:

- "How much is the kitchen used in your home?"
- "Who uses it most?"
- "How many generally sit down at a meal?"
- "How important to you is an eating area in the kitchen?"
- "What kind of cooking do you most enjoy, formal or casual?"
- "How much entertaining do you do?"
- "How do you feel about having a desk in the kitchen area for keeping the grocery list or paying bills?"

Just think creatively. Think through the various appliances and demonstrate any special features, especially things like a super-quiet dishwasher, a disposal, or double ovens with easy controls. If there is a good backyard or a pleasant view from the back, save that for the last part of your demonstration.

If there is any way that you can do it, save the price until last, because you are not selling price. (I'll say this more than once!) Keep in mind that in this situation, money is only one consideration of the many benefits that are establishing value in the mind of the prospect.

SHOWING HOMES AND VILLAS IN THE RIGHT ORDER

Never show properties according to their geographical proximity unless it is absolutely necessary. Your order for showing homes and villas should be determined by their total overall value (like homesites) as follows:

- first: moderate or average, your qualifier home
- second: better than the first in terms of overall value, based on their desires
- third: below average
- fourth: BEST.

There are two different philosophies that work. One is saving the ideal home for last, and the other is showing the ideal home third and then showing the worst example of what they want last so that they will be encouraged to go back and see the ideal home again. Try both of these ways to see which way works best for you. Both of them have their own points of value.

For now, let's save the best for last. Let's assume that you are at your third home. You have dealt with the following basics:

- Started with the front yard and worked your way inside.
- Sincerely demonstrated the features and benefits of the home.
- Observed their reactions carefully.
- Listened to their answers to your questions.
- Gave them breathing space to relax and look around. Don't hover!
- Asked several trial close questions to take their interest temperature.
- Saved the price until last.
- Asked if they could see themselves owning a home like this.

Assuming that number three did not overly appeal to them, and that number two is still in the running, we are on our way to the ideal home. By this time, from all of the answers they've given, you should have a good idea of what they really like and which home should truly be the ideal one. You may have had to change this in mid-stream, which is the reason you must know your inventory very well.

In our industry, one of the oldest sayings is that "Buyers are liars, and sellers don't tell the truth." I'm not sure if that's exactly accurate, but it's a fact that buyers may give you different information once they are in the midst of walking through homes from what you heard sitting in your office. So always have a couple extra "ideal" homes in your pocket that you can switch to if need be.

Compare their lists and yours, and review the likes and dislikes they have had for the previous properties they've seen. Then summarize something like this by referring to the list of their preferences that you've jotted down:

"It sounds like if we could find a home that has…" (naming some of their preferences here)… *That* is the type of home you'd really enjoy. Is that right? All right, that helps me out a lot. Let's see if we can make that happen."

You have learned the type of view they like, the general floor plan that would be functional for them, the kind of construction, price range, and desire for amenities. Now you are ready to position their ideal home in its most favorable light to create the most perceived value.

SHOWING THE IDEAL HOME

Do not overly build up the "ideal home" you are about to show. The last thing you want to do is build up their expectations too high, and then have the home be a let down to them. Take the best route to the home. Pick out a couple of the features in this home that you know they will like, and begin piquing their interest as you are riding toward the home.

Example: "Jason, Ashley, you mentioned that you enjoy entertaining in a casual style. Right? If you had a large, screened-in back porch with its own built-in grill and maybe even a smoker, is that something you would really enjoy?

"You mentioned also that you like having an open, peaceful view, right? What if that screened-in porch had a couple of large paddle fans, a swing, and maybe a couple of rockers and looked out across a beautiful golf fairway? Does that sound like the type of feel you could get used to?"

"Sure!"

"Great! Well, I'm excited about this next home we're about to see. I believe you just may be excited about it, too!"

As you approach the home, do the basics:

- Share stories about the neighbors. (Don't get too personal.)
- Provide testimonials of why others have bought in this particular area.
- Back away and look at the home, landscaping.
- Discuss the site, size, its boundary lines.

Then tantalize a little bit more: "Ashley, you mentioned you like a spacious kitchen, with plenty of storage, didn't you? Be sure and take a close look at those cabinets and pantry when you walk inside!"

When entering a resale home, talk very little. Let them explore and discover with them the various features that they will find appealing. The most important thing you can be doing is to observe their reactions. Some well-placed questions and attentiveness to their answers would be important, but leaving some good silence is just as important.

DEMONSTRATING NEW HOMES

There are some distinct differences between showing a resale and a new home or villa. It is especially important to keep this in mind if you are working for the builder and his homes are the only product that you have to sell.

It has been said that when selling resale property, the agent is "married to the prospect" and can take them to as many different homes as they have to, but when selling a specific new home community, the agent is "married to the product."

As a new home sales specialist, you must listen carefully to any answers from your prospects about their likes, dislikes, goals, and dreams. You must take as many of the features of your new homes as possible and convert them into benefits that will truly fill all these requirements you are hearing. Before you can be effective in selling new homes in a planned community, you must be very knowledgeable not only about the details regarding location, developer, builder, amenities, and competition, but also about the specific features in the individual homes.

In fact, you need to know all of the new home's features so well that you are able to build even more value by getting your prospects excited about things that they never even knew they wanted. It's a matter of taking the little extras and magnifying them.

It's very important in this type of sales environment to keep in mind that just as selling a pie by the slice makes more money than selling the whole pie at once; selling a house feature by feature creates a greater perception of worth. The sum of the parts is greater than the whole! Keep in mind that the biggest competition for a new home is either their existing home, which they may choose to remodel, or another resale home. The real key in selling new homes, especially those yet to be built is to focus on selling tomorrow's values ... today.

Van Rose has a very successful company in eastern Virginia that focuses on new-home sales, and, for the last decade, has averaged well over twelve hundred home sales per year. His seventy salespeople do at least an hour of special training every week. He obviously believes in the fact that knowledge breeds confidence. Not only does he continuously review sales techniques but he also reminds them about the products that they are actually selling.

Why does the builder choose to use a specific type of plywood, shingles, floor coverings, brand-name appliances? The builders that they represent may be using a lot of the same materials that other builders use, but his sales aces have learned how to explain the various components and how they benefit the customers.

Van Rose teaches his people to have their prospects reach to the top of each door and slide their hand across it. "Notice how slick it is? That's because our builder covers all the door edges with polyurethane to seal out any moisture in order to keep the door from warping."

Perhaps a little thing, but little things add up.

Especially, if you remember as the Van Rose people obviously do, to present them in the sales format that we discussed earlier: set up, demo, and close.

DOING IT RIGHT

I was working once with a sales ace named Judy. I asked her if she would be willing to give me her presentation of her new model. Even though she had been quite successful, there were places Judy could have improved. She did a great job of showing me their homes but could have added more value if she had taken some of the features and sold them as benefits.

She was showing me the foyer and opened a very spacious coat closet. As she was demonstrating the size of this closet and its location, my eye caught a spigot-like valve in the back left corner.

"What's that?" I asked.

"Oh, that's just the master valve for the water," she said.

"You mean I can shut off all the water coming into this home by turning that valve?"

"Yep!"

Apparently, Judy had never had water spraying everywhere while she was searching frantically all over the front and back yards, crawling under a spider-infested crawlspace trying to find that elusive shut-off valve!

Think of the difference it may have if she had demonstrated this little feature something like this:

Judy (before opening the closet door): "Terry, have you ever had to deal with a burst pipe with water spraying everywhere and then realized, 'I have no idea where to shut off this water'?" (The set up.)

Terry: "Yeah, I sure have!"

Judy: "How did you feel?"

Terry: "Frustrated, irritated....even a little stupid!"

Judy: "This builder believes that convenience should be one of the most important aspects of a new home." (She opens the closet door.) "See that valve in the corner? Why don't you step over and turn it three times? You have just shut off every drop of water coming into this house." (The demo.) "Thinking ahead about little things like that could make a big difference in the enjoyment of the home, couldn't it?" (The close.)

Did you see the set up, demo, and close?

It takes a little longer this way, but real selling takes longer than telling. *Selling is interactive, while telling is simply a monologue.*

This format may not be used with every feature you are pointing out, but should be used with the ones where you want to make a lasting impact.

SELLING FROM BLUEPRINTS

Believe it or not, it is easier to sell something that is not there rather than to sell a finished product. Imagination is always greater than reality. With a finished product the prospect gets only what they see, but with the unfinished one they get what they imagine. And the imagination is guided by the words that you use to paint the proper picture in their mind's eye.

I highly recommend John Trent and Gary Smalley's superb book *The Language of Love*. It deals with the power of communicating through the use of word pictures. They refer to studies done by Robert Hoffman (*Annals of the New York Academy of Science*, December 1984, pp. 137–166) which conclude that our brains actually work faster and use up more energy when we are hearing a word picture or story than when we are reading or listening to conventional words.

That is the reason that selling from a blueprint requires some creative thought and good communication skills. You would be much more effective if through the use of "active" words you convert the two-dimensional blueprint into a three-dimensional picture in their mind's eye.

Here's an example of *telling:* "As you can see, you have an open kitchen right next to the family room."

This is an example of *selling:* "You mentioned you enjoy entertaining. Where do most of the people seem to like to congregate at a party? Probably near the kitchen, right? This floor plan has been designed to comfortably accommodate that. See the two doors on the far side of the kitchen? These open into the family room, and this counter, away from the cooking area and sink, is a pass-through to the dining and family room area.

"When the people are milling around the table, standing around the counter, and even passing through the kitchen, the traffic flows smoothly without ever creating congestion. Besides that, the one working in the kitchen doesn't feel left out. Right?

"Can you see the layout of the kitchen and family rooms unfold? You can almost feel the excitement of the party, can't you?"

The primary keys to successfully selling from blueprints are as follows:

- Use active words in describing what's taking place in the space you're showing
- Ask questions that require involvement, such as:
  "How do you feel about the location of the deck?"
  "Do you like the idea of this wraparound deck, or would you prefer a screened porch?"

Properly demonstrating homes or villas is quite involved. There's a lot more to it than walking through, pointing over to a room, and saying, "This is the kitchen." Most of our buyers can figure that out. What they need from you is voicing that deeper message, the one below the surface that explains how they will enjoy and benefit from these different features. Think "dermis," not "epidermis"!

Always ask yourself, "Am I selling, or am I telling?"

It's not how many hours you put in, but what you put into the hours that count.
— T. L. Weaver

9

WHAT REALLY MOTIVATES PEOPLE TO DECIDE?

One afternoon I was wandering through a mountain antique shop. I say "antique," although frankly, most of the stuff looked like pure junk to me. Keep in mind that one person's trash is another person's treasure.

I happened to see an aeronautical sign which was really just an old piece of wood about two feet high by three feet wide. To me, that looked like a pretty good piece of firewood, but the price on it was $1250. Pretty expensive firewood, huh?

I asked the shopkeeper about it. "Oh," he said, "these signs are very popular among flyers who collect flying memorabilia."

All of us have been in galleries that display artwork that looks more like rejects from a second-grade art contest. Yet it sells for thousands or millions of dollars. Why? Because they were painted by "master" artists, and the buyers were convinced that they were great values. But are they great values?

Of course! It's simple economics: supply and demand. There's a limited supply and large demand from enough people with money who felt that ownership of one of these things would enhance their status, self-esteem, enjoyment, or whatever.

We've all heard "Beauty lies in the eye of the beholder." So does value. As we mentioned earlier, there is no real value in anything on this earth except for people. Everything else has a value placed on it based on the individual's core values. What's valuable to the prospect?

Perception of Value. When *value perception* is heightened in the mind of the prospect, it automatically triggers the *desire to acquire* or possess that which is valuable; therefore, the real key to successful sales is to develop personal perceived value. There are a number of ways we can do this:

1. Have a clear understanding of what represents value to your prospect. It is not always related to money.
2. Always speak in terms of the benefits of owning in your community.
3. Make subtle comparison of values to other communities that tend to be your primary competition.
4. Provide numerous strong third-party testimonials.
5. Show a nice (possibly leather) binder that contains pictures and letters from your purchasers. Include pictures of community activities.
6. Set up and utilize community ambassadors. These are the gung-ho owners who would enjoy and do a good job of taking your best prospects out for dinner, golfing, and so forth.
7. Learn to use a video camera in an effective way. It's an excellent follow-up tool. As you are videoing the one-of-a-kind property for them, make it fun and talk directly to them as if they were standing right beside you. Keep it light and entertaining. Having a digital camera is a given. That follow up picture that you e-mailed is quite effective, and it's good for them to hear your voice on the video.
8. Make sure all other departments within your organization are working together. Whether their responsibility is security, food and beverage, or golf, he or she is a salesperson who is assisting you in selling real estate. After all, that's what keeps the doors open. They need to be trained to think this way. A rude or careless comment or action from them can destroy in seconds what you have spent hours and even days building!
9. Generate more physical, and consequently more emotional, involvement with the prospect such as boat rides, shrimping, fishing, hiking, golfing, or skiing. Give them a taste of what life in your community would be like.
10. Remember to sell the various aspects of your community "by the slice."

Finally, once the desire to acquire these values begins to take place, another emotion automatically kicks in: FEAR.

What we're talking about here is fear on the part of the prospective buyer of losing out on something that he/she has begun to perceive as valuable.

WHAT REALLY MOTIVATES PEOPLE TO DECIDE?

It can be one of your most powerful tools for making a sale.

USING FEAR AS A TOOL

It is human nature to want something more if we know other people want it, too. Maybe all of us are afflicted with a little bit of greed. The true sales ace will learn to subtly play on and enhance this fear, knowing that this fear of losing out sparks a *sense of urgency to act*. Most of the time if there is no urgency, there is no action. How do we develop and capitalize on the fear of loss?

You have found out what the prospects want to accomplish. You have discovered what their deep buying motives (or their hot buttons) really are.

Then you emphasize dollar values. Explain clearly how values have risen in the recent past. Kiawah Island sales ace Cynthia Bettridge has a super technique for demonstrating values.

She calls it "map overlays." She uses three or four maps representing each of the last three or four years. She marks in different colors for each map a number of examples of properties that have been purchased and the prices that were paid. She starts with the oldest map by describing the prices in that year and pointing out examples that have been marked. Then she moves to the next year, showing the escalation of prices in various areas of the Island.

According to Cynthia, "It really helps establish credibility. The prospect doesn't feel what's being said is just a lot of fluff because they can actually see the records."

Indicate the scarcity of your property to your prospects. Let them know that a lot of people want the very same things they want. This would be a good time to use articles, such as "How to Beat the Boomer Rush" in *Fortune* magazine's Special Edition, October 1997. There are also some great real estate articles in Harry Dent's book *The Roaring 2000s: Building the Wealth and Life Style You Desire in the Greatest Boom in History.*

Tell your prospects about marketing incentives that may be offered for a limited time, including natural ones such as low-interest rates and financing availability in addition to internally-created benefits such as limitations on building permits or club memberships. The aim, of course, is to create a bandwagon effect and everybody's getting involved.

Be sure they get the sense that something is happening, which will add to a sense of urgency to act. One of the biggest mistakes I see developers make is having too much inventory on the market. This destroys the ability to create a sense of urgency. I've seen salespeople give out price lists that have one hundred or more pieces of property on them with all the prices listed. If you're going to give out any kind of price list, it should have price ranges instead of individual property prices.

"Purchased" signs should at least be on a site map in the office if not on the sites. The buyer must be made aware (through stories interwoven in conversation after meeting the prospects) of others who have hesitated and lost. They either lost out on their ideal property or had to settle for their second choice, or they lost money because they purchased after a price increase.

The more the perceived value, the stronger the desire to acquire it. The stronger the desire to acquire it, the greater the fear of losing it. The greater the fear of losing it, the more intense the sense of urgency to act.

The more intense the sense of urgency, the more likely they are to decide to buy. And when that happens, *everybody wins*!

It's all right to look back in life — but never get caught staring too long.
— T. L. Weaver

CLOSING THE CLOSE ONES

Sinking that ten-foot putt to win the tournament! Tagging home plate with the winning run! Stripping the net, with only two seconds remaining, to win the championship! Catching that pass for the winning touchdown!

All of these created a win in the books, but none of them actually won the game. Winning the game resulted from an intricate combination of well-executed offensive strategies, actions, and decisions coupled with focused concentration on not making dumb mistakes.

Closing a sale is much the same. That mental decision to buy and filling out the agreement is simply the culmination of your work, an intricate combination of offensive maneuvers (without being offensive) and correct actions coupled with not making dumb mistakes.

Assuming you've done your work, it is now time to begin moving into the fourth phase of the sale, the closing.

At this point, the amateur salesperson tends to come across as too direct, appears hungry for the sale, and creates an atmosphere of tension and pressure. He may ask questions such as: "Is this what you want to buy?" "Do you want to make an offer on it?" "Can I go ahead and write this one up?"

No wonder he does not feel he is able to close more than once without turning off or irritating the prospect. He lets his nerves and ignorance show!

The sales ace exudes an air of relaxed confidence because he or she knows how to handle any situation that may arise. In addition, because a sales ace cares more about what's best for the prospect than simply about the commission, there isn't the same do-or-die pressure.

This air of confidence will at times create just that extra bit of momentum needed for a buying atmosphere that will assist the prospect over the decision threshold.

Trial closing, or temperature questions, is designed to test the prospect's feelings *before* the mental decision to buy has actually been made. After walking the site and asking those questions and receiving positive responses, the next logical step would be to discuss the price.

The prospects may have asked earlier about the price, even as they were approaching the property. The amateur salesperson would answer at their first inquiry, but this is not the best way. Every professional salesperson selling any product will present the features and benefits of their product before telling the price. Why should real estate be any different? Since you are the one in control, you decide when the price is disclosed.

How do you answer the price question if it comes up before it should? The following are some examples:

- "Tell you what, Jason and Ashley, let's take a quick look at it first just to see if you even like it. If you don't, it doesn't really matter what it costs, does it?"
- "Come on, Jason and Ashley, you know how we salespeople are. We always save the best part for last."
- "We'll save that for a surprise. Let's take a look at it first so you can decide if it's a good or a bad surprise."

Each of these should be delivered in light and relaxed, almost kidding manner. Keep the whole process fun, but stay in control. It's better for prices to be given once value has been established in their minds. Ideally, the perceived values will outweigh the price.

Remember: *People buy value that they can envision.*

The feeling everybody wants to experience when buying almost anything is that they are getting more than what they are paying for. This is true for purchasing clothing, cars, or property. You must create this if you expect to close successfully.

How do you do it? We have already discussed some of the ways such as presenting the benefits, pointing out numerous other properties that have been purchased, testimonials of what others felt about the values, the order of properties demonstrated and the way price is built up before being revealed. This price build up is assuming that the ideal property is indeed a superior value to the other properties that have been seen.

If you have done your job correctly by creating value, the prospects will be expecting the price to be considerably higher. After all, they expect you to move them up past their limit the way most salespeople do. The prospects should have been writing descriptions on their pads of each property they have seen. Take a look at some of the descriptions:

- "Let's just review what we've seen. The first house (or property) had A and B that you liked, but it didn't have C or D and it was five hundred thousand dollars."
- "Most folks would figure that homes like this which have A, B, C and D (features and benefits) would be at least five hundred fifty thousand dollars, but it is only four hundred eighty-five. That's very reasonable, isn't it?"

JUST RELAX

If the majority of their answers are positive, then you are ready to proceed smoothly with the close. Moving into the close from the demonstration must be one continual process, not jerky and uncertain. Keep your verbal pace and volume the same as before. If you have ever acted relaxed, now is the time!

But how do you relax if you are uptight?

All actors on Broadway deal with butterflies just before the curtain rises. Top athletes are uptight before the big games. Speakers are nervous before facing an audience, but they force themselves to act and look relaxed.

So the first thing to do is to try sitting down.

People tend to prefer to sit down when making big decisions. So, have a seat. If you are at a homesite, then your car would work, maybe a nearby clubhouse, or even a picnic table. If you are in a home or villa, then go to the family room or the kitchen table.

Lean back. Relax! Create the casual atmosphere that "it's no big deal" by having an attitude of: "It's entirely up to you. It doesn't make a bit of difference to me. It's your decision."

Don't drag it out. The most painful part is getting across that mental buying bump in the road. Don't be like the guy who walked into the dentist and asked how much he would charge to pull a bad tooth.

"Fifty dollars," said the dentist.

"Gosh," said the guy. "How long will it take?"

"About a minute or two," said the dentist.

"That's a lot of money for only a minute or two of work."

The dentist looked at him and said, "If it's the amount of time that's bothering you, I'll take as much time pulling the tooth as you want."

If you are dealing with real prospects who want to accomplish something, and you have found an ideal place for them, rest assured they want to move through the clouds of uncertainty and indecision as quickly and comfortably as they possibly can. They may not let you know this. In fact, they may need you to navigate them through the clouds.

Imagine for a moment that you are an ace fighter pilot getting ready to taxi your F-18 jet fighter down the runway. As you push the throttle forward, you are building up more speed and momentum. Imagine, also, that as you are moving down the runway, you are going past a flag about every fifty yards. Each of these flags represents a question. Each question is getting more and more specific about their true feelings about this site. The last question is the one about value or price: "So the value for this homesite is one hundred twenty thousand, which is quite reasonable, isn't it?"

If you are receiving positive answers to the majority of these questions, including the final one, create a reason to leave them alone for a couple of minutes. You must give them "room to buy." Like this: "Well, folks, it looks like we've found something that's quite attractive to you. Why don't I give you a chance to chat about it for a while, and I'll call to make sure it's still available before you get too excited about it. I'll also get my calculator to go over some numbers with you."

At this point, go to your car and make the call. After all, another agreement could have been written on it within the previous couple of hours.

Return after a minute or so, but if your prospects have quickly left the site, or are preparing to leave the home, they are not ready to be closed or make a decision. Their interest level is obviously not high enough. You must find out what concerns or problems they are facing, and then find the right property for them.

Let's assume for now that everything is falling into place. As you walk over with the pad and calculator, observe them and listen to what they're saying. If they are talking, don't interrupt. If they are taking in the view, be quiet. If they ask you a question, answer it clearly.

Back to our analogy. You are in your F-18 fighter jet, moving faster and faster down the runway. All of a sudden, you realize that there is a problem ahead. There is a huge bombed-out crater in the middle of the runway. You are heading right for it. What are you going to do? Obviously, you're going to push the throttle forward all the way, pull the joystick back, and lift off the runway to fly safely over the danger.

Now, move this analogy into your selling world. As the plane began moving down the runway, it was passing one flag after another, which represented *trial close questions*. Keep in mind that these are questions that can be answered *before* their decision to purchase has been made. This bomb crater is where all the buyer's objections are hiding. To just move faster and faster toward the edge and then try to slow down through the use of some typical amateurish questions like, "Well, do you want to make an offer," or "Shall I just write it up for you?" creates a risk. An objection might come up out that crater and pull you in.

It may be an objection such as, "We'll just have to think about it," or, "We'll have to talk to our attorney or accountant about it," etc. The safest way to avoid this is a way that requires more guts and confidence. It is to throw the throttle forward, pull back the joystick (with a relaxed, laid-back attitude), and lift up over the crater with the use of *closing questions*.

WHAT ARE CLOSING QUESTIONS?

The prospect's answer regarding his feelings or the actions he desires to take can only be accurately given *after* the mental decision has been made!

You begin by expressing the availability of the property and going over the payments on your pad. For example, "Good news, folks! It's still available. Let me just show you what we are looking at payment-wise to make sure you feel comfortable with everything. This site is one hundred twenty thousand dollars. Most folks finance 80 percent, but you could finance less if you wanted to. But, with an 80 percent loan, it would be twenty-four thousand dollars as a down payment."

Proceed to explain the financing arrangement and circle the monthly payment when you come to it. "Does that feel comfortable to you?"

If the answer is "Yes", or "Well, we would probably just pay cash," then continue to move forward, ever higher with the throttle (your words) and pushing forward by asking closing questions that can be answered only if their decision to purchase has been made (or is very close). Try questions like:

- "How are you thinking about situating your home to take best advantage of the view?"
- "Now, would you be building a one- or two-story home?"
- "Are you going to need any recommendations for an architect or builder?"
- "Are you going to be doing all of your own decorating?"
- "Would you like for me to recommend a couple of good decorators to give you some ideas to get you started?"
- "Tell you what, why don't we just sit down and let me explain how we do business so there's no confusion."

The answer to a closing question can only be answered truthfully after the decision to buy has been made. Now, move them forward, keeping in mind that the most important thing that must happen is for them to have mentally crossed over that buying line. As you are moving toward the area where you will go over the paperwork, casually throw in statements such as: "Jason, Ashley, it's really going to be good having you as a part of our community. You're going to really love it here."

As you sit down, simply pull out an Agreement or a Reservation sheet, and move into it. One of the biggest fears most salespeople have is forcing that pen to touch the paper before actually hearing the prospects say they want the property. If you wait to hear that, you've probably waited too long to close. They actually have closed you.

Here is a simple, easy way to learn how to move into your agreement forcefully, yet smoothly. It's called the Sample Close, and it's almost like using training wheels.

THE SAMPLE CLOSE

As you are spreading out your Reservation or Purchasing Agreement, pleasantly state: "Let's just assume for the time being that this is the right home site for you.

This is the Purchase Agreement that we'll use. Let's just put 'Sample' on it, and go through it to see if you have any questions."

Write SAMPLE in big letters across the front page. Break eye contact with the prospect and look at the agreement. Then,, with pen in hand, begin with broad general questions like the following:

- "What is your home address?"
- "Would you be taking title in both of your names?"
- "What are your middle initials?"

Casually, but not too neatly, fill out the agreement. Save the price until last. If you are selling developer property, simply proceed as long as you are getting positive responses.

If your ideal property is a resale and some negotiations would be in order, proceed just as before, stating and writing up a full price offer. You will probably meet some resistance if you have a bona fide purchaser. He or she may say, "Wait a minute; I'm not going to offer the asking price."

You have arrived where you wanted to be.

When the prospect states that he or she is unwilling to offer the full price, an offer is at least in its embryonic stage. Do not immediately respond with, "Well, how much *do* you want to offer?"

Make a couple of attempts to justify the value of the asking price. Let the prospect know that negotiating is not always the order of the day here. After all, you are probably working for the seller. Finally you can ask, "Well, Jason, what price *do* you have in mind?"

Attempt to get the offer up as high as possible to one that might be accepted without a counter. A large number of transactions fall apart during nitpicky negotiations. It becomes the principle of the thing that often destroys negotiations. After the Sample Agreement is complete, say "Let me go over this with you to make sure it's correct."

Go back through it verbally as they look on, and continue: "Everything is pretty clear, isn't it? Fine. Why don't I write this more neatly so that it can be read? While I'm doing that, why don't you make your earnest money check out to Ace Realty for ten thousand dollars? I'm excited for you folks. It's going to be great having you as neighbors!"

This approach to closing takes knowledge, confidence, and courage, but it's the best way in the long run.

OBJECTION VERSUS REJECTION

But what if the decision does not arrive quite this smoothly? What should you do?

In the first place, do you know that most salespeople actually receive very few objections? In fact, they usually don't get turned down by prospective buyers.

According to the late Dave Stone, noted authority on new home sales, an extensive study revealed that 65 percent of the people who had not purchased a home in the studied area stated that they were never even asked to purchase.

What does this mean? Why should a salesperson take his or her valuable time, work with prospects for hours, days, even weeks and not even attempt to close the people on making a decision? After all, would the prospect honestly want to spend that much of his or her time, unless he or she wanted to accomplish something?

I am sure you are a lot of fun to be with, but most people could think of a few things more rewarding to do than just riding around looking at property all day or all week with you.

One of the reasons for reluctance on the salesperson's part is because of the emotion with which we all must deal and overcome: *fear of rejection.*

The amateur confuses an objection to the offer with a personal rejection. Since none of us likes personal rejection, the surest guarantee against facing it is avoidance, so that is exactly what the amateur does. He or she has worked like crazy by showing a potential customer property after property, taking them to lunch, patiently putting up with their sucker-licking kids, dutifully reporting for duty whenever they discover another property that they just have to see.

The amateur gives it everything and waits patiently like a dog for a bone for the prospect to say "This is it! Write it up!"

When the amateur doesn't hear this famous closing phrase, he or she often folds: "Sure enjoyed meeting and working with you folks. If I can ever help you with anything around here, just let me know."

They think it's better to leave it that way with the prospects thinking, "What a nice/delightful guy (or lady)," than it is for them to feel they are being roped into a close. The amateur thinks, "They are going to be back, and I am sure they will want to work with me."

How many cards or computer records do we all have with the names of prospects like that? Many people will come back, but whether you do it now or later, you'll still have to close them and not wait for them to close you – if they're ever going to be anything more than prospects.

So why not do it now?

As a manager, make it your business to build your people,
and they in turn will build your business.
— T. L. Weaver

CONQUERING THE FEAR OF REJECTION

We have an innate desire to be approved of and accepted by other human beings. The degree of that need for approval in an individual's life is primarily based on two things: his or her basic personality makeup and the feedback received from parents and others in the first five formative years of life.

If a person encounters much rejection from significant others throughout his life, the natural reaction is to start seeing himself as unacceptable. Just as real estate has value based on comparisons of other pieces of properties, so we as human beings tend to establish our self-worth by comparing ourselves to others' accomplishments, looks, or skills.

Here is where the real danger sets in. The external rejection begins transforming into a much more dangerous form of rejection, the internal rejection. When a person starts internalizing self-rejection, if it's not stopped it becomes a downward spiral. It's mighty difficult for a person to be up on anyone or anything else when he's down on himself.

Depending on how far down the spiral a person has gone, he or she may stop this trend, either with professional counseling if the downward spiral is advanced, or by using proper self talk. When you get fed up with negative self-esteem brought on by the wrong internal thinking from external rejections, stand up, stare at yourself in the mirror, and have a good, long counseling session with yourself. After all, psychologists say that the best counselor is the one living inside of you. Look yourself in the eye and say out loud with total complete conviction:

- "You are a unique being created by an all-powerful God!"
- "You have been given special gifts and talents! They are there, even if they haven't shown up just yet!"
- "You are going to start thinking about how you can benefit others around you, and get your mind off yourself and your concern about what others think!"
- "You will start counting your blessings and stop cursing your problems!"
- "You are a good person with integrity, and you will refuse to listen to anything that tries to contradict this truth!"
- "You are going to start taking on little challenges and overcome the fears that have kept you captive in the past!"

Now, aren't you feeling better already? After you have done this, do it again. And again! And again!

A miracle probably won't happen. You probably won't feel or see a significant change at the moment. But the change is taking place.

That's where faith comes in. It will be a fight. Nothing of great value has ever come easily, and helping improve your self-esteem is of great value.

There's a funny, crazy movie that Tillie and I have probably seen a dozen times. It is called *What About Bob?,* starring Bill Murray and Richard Dreyfuss. I encourage you to see it. As crazy as it is, it has some good psychological truths about how to defeat neurosis and poor self-esteem. Its therapy is based on baby steps, or taking on little challenges and developing a pattern of success, and then moving on to larger challenges.

Baby steps are the little accomplishments that serve as building blocks for greater achievements down the road. It's just as simple as it sounds. Believe me, it works. If you never make yourself do at least some things that you fear, you will never grow to be any greater than what you already are.

Think of the young sophomore in high school whose sole desire was to play basketball. He worked hard for years. He gave it all he had during that first week of practice before the cut was to take place. The big day came to see who made the team. As he stood with his best friend, staring at the list on the gym door, he realized that he had not made it. He had been cut from the team.

It absolutely devastated him. When he got home and told his mom, they both broke down and had a big cry together.

This young man was at a crucial point in his life. He could let this event totally destroy him and give up on the game he loved, or he could choose to use the experience as a motivating force toward higher goals.

At the end of the season, he got up enough nerve to ask the coach if he could ride on the bus to the district tournament with the team. The coach said that the only way he could go was to carry the other players' bags. That's exactly what he did.

When he walked into the gymnasium and looked up and saw his parents who had come to see the tournament, he realized that at first they thought he had been given a chance to play.

He said, "When I saw the look on their faces as they saw me carrying the other guys' bags, I decided to be the best basketball player I possibly could be."

He said that feeling of deep disappointment from being rejected from his team was "good" because he knew he never wanted to experience that feeling again. So he decided to use this *dis*appointment and transform it into *his* appointment for future achievement. He turned his rejection into his objective, which turned his problem into his purpose.

I think we would all agree that the world of basketball (and sports overall) is a lot better off because Michael Jordan chose to use this experience as a stepping stone, not as a stumbling block.

He chose to see it not as a rejection of himself as a person, but an objection to his current level of skill at playing basketball — something he could do a lot about.

Rejection? No, you'll never love it. But you don't have to loathe it, either. Learn to use it. Let it build the pressure inside that will propel you to greater heights!

The opposite of the fear of rejection is the feeling of security. How is real security developed? I am sure there are many ways, but I believe there is a fundamental method common to all people who have internal security. Real security comes as a result of one's willingness to take on challenges and overcome the natural fears (rejection!) and uncertainties that accompany those challenges.

How does the high-dive champion master a skill that scares the willies out of most of us? Did the diver begin with a ten-meter board? Hardly! How about at the edge of the pool? Then, step by step, higher and higher, he or she climbed.

Inner security is built the same way. It involves facing fear, learning what it takes to overcome it, and then being willing to move right on through it.

It has been said that courage is simply "fear that has said its prayers." Courage is also a decision to face that fear and let it work for you. Someone once asked me how I get rid of the butterflies before I get up in front of a group to speak.

I replied, "Oh, I don't try to get rid of the butterflies. I simply try to get them to line up and fly in formation."

Your job, or at least part of it, is to face rejection and develop inner security. Now, add to this what a wise man once said, "The reason many people don't recognize opportunity is because it comes disguised wearing work clothes."

CRISIS!

Actual rejection may feel like a crisis in your life. It might produce more than a little lack of self-esteem. But let's look at what crisis really means.

If you look at the Chinese word for crisis, you'll see that it is made up of two symbols which state the situation exactly. If taken separately, the two symbols mean "danger" and "opportunity." Taken together, the symbols mean "crisis."

There is danger and risk in our work. But there is also the unlimited opportunity for advancement. Whichever you focus on will determine the *outcome*, and that will most certainly determine your income.

What truly counts in life is not how long you live—but what lives long after you.
— T. L. Weaver

$$12$$

THE CORRECT ATTITUDE FOR CLOSING

Luck is when opportunity and preparation meet.

It has been said before that *attitude* far more than aptitude determines your altitude in sales. The closing ace understands that people will be more persuaded by the depth of his conviction than by the height of his logic.

What attitude is necessary? You need to have a heartfelt, sincere belief that what you have is the best thing for the price for your customer. This belief will give you the power of persuasion to become an ace closer.

You also need to understand the big difference between manipulating and motivating. This is important, because the persuasive techniques you will be encouraged to use could become simple manipulation in the hands of the wrong person.

Some amateur salespeople are reluctant to use the techniques of persuasion for fear that they may be perceived as manipulating people. They have a faulty understanding of what professional selling really is. They haven't learned and accepted the fact that successful selling has a direct relation to unselfish service.

Manipulation is an "I win, you lose" attitude, or doing what's best for *me*. But motivation is a "we both win" attitude by doing what's best for *you*.

Obviously, there are people in our industry who exaggerate the truth, think only about their commission, and see each prospect simply as a "mark" who just needs to be sold something. These people are manipulators of others. Yes, there are plenty of these people, and many of them make big bucks, but they miss out on the psychological rewards they could have as a result of positively impacting people's lives, building lasting relationships, and reaping the rewards of numerous referrals.

The correct attitude for being an ace closer involves:

- *giving* prospects an advantage by becoming property owners, not a feeling that you're *taking* advantage of them
- providing a *service*, not pushing for a *sale*
- choosing to *face* rejection, not *fearing* rejection
- a message to the *heart,* not just to the *head*
- use of *word pictures,* not just *technical jargon*
- *listening* intently to them, not just *talking* at them
- being *light and relaxed,* not *intense and serious*
- speaking *low and slow,* not *loud and fast*
- being *empathetic* with, not *sympathetic* to, their feelings.

Just as the proper key unlocks a certain door, so the proper key in closing lies in determining the true motives and desires of your prospect. How? With thoughtful, probing questions and deep attentive listening.

WHY DON'T MORE SALESPEOPLE CLOSE?

Many salespeople don't close sales because they don't understand what professional closing is all about. Many have personally experienced the vise-like feeling of being in the hands of an amateur salesperson.

They promptly promise themselves that they will never do that to anybody. What they fail to understand is that *closing is not something you do to people. It's something you do for them.*

The true sales ace is the one who is more compassion-oriented than commission-motivated. Everyone wants to earn a good income, but the real pro sincerely believes that the prospect does want to accomplish something. The sales ace feels that if no decision is made, the prospect will lose out on far more than he or she will.

The ace salesperson also knows that if he or she helps enough prospects accomplish what they want, his or her needs and wants will be more than met. A wise person once said that "non-persistent salespeople raise very skinny kids."

It is better to be persistent and prosperous than passive and poor.

Why is there a need for helping the prospect in the decision-making process? Why doesn't the prospect just see the light and say, "That's it! Write it up"?

The reason is simple: FEAR! They are fearful of making a wrong decision. All kinds of thoughts and concerns surface in their minds. Just as the corn starts to pop when the oil gets hot, so do latent worries, doubts and fears start popping up as the prospects feel themselves getting hotter on a certain property.

How are these fears manifested during an otherwise smooth sale? Do the prospects just look up with sheer terror in their eyes and confess, "I'm afraid of making this decision. I may be messing up!"

No way! We are all taught not to be afraid or admit our fears. "Go into your room," we hear as children. "The dark won't hurt you!" Or, as we hear as our knees knock while standing on our first two-meter board: "Come on, you can do it — dive in! Don't be afraid!"

Many of our prospects experience these same types of fears. To them, purchasing this property may be like looking into the dark room of their futures, or being reminded of others who dove in over their heads. What do we hear when these fears rear their ugly heads? We hear a lot of sophisticated reasons for delay (most of which are impostors) such as:

- "We need to think about it."
- "We don't make decisions without sleeping on them."
- "We need to talk this over with our accountant, lawyer, brother-in-law…"
- "The price is just too high."

How the salesperson responds verbally and visually to such objections will, to a large extent, determine the success or failure of the sale. The amateur takes it personally and interprets this objection as rejection. The facial expression, which up to this point has been a pleasant smile, begins to slip away. The posture becomes more erect. The neck becomes a little red. The air of sweet confidence, which had surrounded him or her, begins to transform into beads of perspiration. The eyes begin to squint, and fangs emerge from the mouth.

Before the prospect's very own eyes, this pleasant, mild-mannered, compassionate servant of sales they felt they could count on transforms into … *Count Closer!*

The problem lies in the fact that the only thing this salesperson is counting at that point is the commission dollars that will be lost instead of the benefits the prospects will be missing. His focus is all wrong, and it shows.

Here again, we have a misunderstanding of persuasion in the close. When the amateur hears the objection, he or she feels like the objection must be countered and shown to be wrong or invalid. This attempt jerks the salesperson away from the buyer's side where the role of "assistant buyer" has been played, over to the opposite side, to where the "selling hat" is placed firmly on his or her head. In physics, for every action, there is an equal and opposite reaction. In sales, *for every obvious attempt to sell, there is an equal and opposite resistance to buy.*

In fact, even the air begins to change from charming to chilly, from acceptance to antagonism. Why does this happen? It happens because the amateur does not understand that to be successful in closing in a persuasive way; the salesperson must *learn to comfort, not to confront.*

PROVIDING COMFORT

Picture a small boy trying to reach the light switch to illuminate a dark room. He calls for you and asks for your help. You enter the room and he explains to you that he is afraid of the dark. Do you look down on him like a towering giant and say: "What's the matter? Are you chicken or something?" I don't think so.

But if you kneel on one knee so that you are at his level, look him straight in the eye, and say: "Jefferson, I can understand exactly how you feel. I remember very clearly when I was about your age and I had to sleep in my room by myself. I, too, was a little scared at first because those shadows in my room scared me. Then my dad came over, turned the light on, and showed me there was nothing there to hurt me. After that, I was never afraid to go into my room again."

People need to be comforted and encouraged at times of doubt or fear, not confronted. Confrontation just makes them act even more irrational. Dave Stone once said, "People have to feel good about themselves when they are about to make a major decision, regardless of who they are or how much money they have."

So what do we do? We must first recognize the emptiness of most objections. They are like smoke. They are used as shields to camouflage the fear of deciding. If ignored, they will often go away. If the objection is valid, it will come up a second time, and then it can be dealt with.

"With long forbearance, and calmness of spirit, a judge or ruler (or real estate prospect!) is persuaded and soft words break down the most bone-like resistance (Proverbs 25:15, parenthetical comment by Weaver.)

126

MORE BODY LANGUAGE

Upon receiving an objection for the **first time,** the sales ace shows the following body language:

Posture	Relaxed
Expression	Looks pleasant and understanding, with a relaxed smile
Voice	Speaks at a moderate pace, with a soft, sincere tone
Eyes	Gazes directly into their eyes, with sincerity and compassion

Then empathize with them and *ignore* the objection: "I can appreciate how you feel. I wouldn't want you to think about buying this home unless you felt comfortable with it and that it is the right thing to do. By the way, I almost neglected to show you Feature X." The sales ace has held back a couple of features and benefits for this very moment.

Or he says, "I know just how you feel. If you don't like it, don't you dare get it. By the way..."

Adjust the words to your personality. But you get the idea. Let me remind you of something. If you don't get objections, you won't get sales. Many objections are merely signs of interest. Interpret those objections as questions or requests for additional information.

For instance, when people say they need to think about it, you might interpret this as "Give me enough additional information and emotional benefit to convince me that the value of this property to my family and my life is just too good to pass up." Or, if they say they have to talk with an accountant, a brother-in-law, or anyone else, hear them saying, "Give me enough information to convince me that I'm making a wise decision without having to get someone else's opinion." Hear these objections for what they really are, a cry for help.

Once you have given the empathetic phrase, get up if you're sitting down. Get some physical action going and start getting excited about this additional benefit you're about to show.

This benefit needs to be significant enough to add some weight to the buying side of the balance in the prospect's mind. Remember, their pile of cash is on one side of the scale, and your features and benefits of this property are on the other. At some point, the scale will tip in your favor if there are enough benefits.

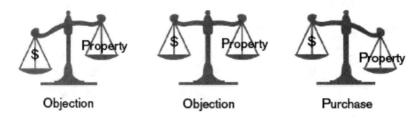

| Objection | Objection | Purchase |

GIVING AWAY THE FARM

The amateur may give it all away at the beginning. The ace will hold back a few things. What do I mean about holding back certain features or benefits? There may be a bonus room above the garage that they haven't seen yet. Perhaps there is an awesome trout stream just down at the other end of the yard one hundred feet away that they haven't seen. Perhaps you can walk to the beach in five minutes and you'll be able to show them what a pleasant stroll it is. Be creative and think. If you haven't held back some features, and you choose to wait and try a close after you've explained everything, you'll be like the gunslinger who shot all six of his bullets and missed. Then the person he's facing aims straight at him and blows him away. Save some of your bullets!

After an enthusiastic demonstration of the additional benefit, the sales ace will slowly bring the prospects back to the matter at hand by asking some more temperature questions. This helps to get the prospects into a *yes* mode of thinking.

At this time, the ace will implement a slight "take away" technique by using a Crossroads Close.

CROSSROADS CLOSE

Sales Ace: "Jason and Ashley, if I might be so bold, could I suggest something? If this home does not have the necessary features and won't fill the bill as the right place for you, let's forget about it and find one that will. But, if it does, then let's move on with it before someone else does.

Sales Ace: "Let me ask you this. If you believed in your own minds that this was the right home for you, would you want to proceed with it?"

Prospect: "Well, if we believed it was."

Sales Ace: "Well, let's see if we can determine that. Probably the best way would be to look back at our original goal. Let's pull out our dream list that we put together and see if this home fits."

Get the list of requirements which you've written down earlier during the initial interview or during the discovery presentation. Do not just start checking off each one of these. Get into a position where the prospects can also see the lists. You will be taking each item on the list and converting it into two or three positive responses. Remember, it's the little yeses that make the big difference. For example:

Sales Ace: "Jason and Ashley, you said that you wanted a scenic open view of the golf course, right?"

Prospect: "Right."

Sales Ace: "Let's get up and take another look at this view." Get up and move to the best view. "Do you feel that this type of view would suit you?" (Or, "How do you feel about this view?")

Prospect: "It's super!"

Sales Ace (Point with the pen.): "Do you feel we could check this one off?"

Prospect: "Yes."

Go through each item in a similar fashion. You must be very humble, soft-spoken, nonchalant, confident, encouraging, positive, and relaxed. *This must not ever come across as entrapment, but rather as encouragement.*

After you have completed the list analysis, look the prospect in the eye, smile, and give a positive affirmation of succeeding at the goal such as, "Well, it looks like your decision has been made for you, doesn't it? Let's put it on paper and see how it looks."

Or: "Looks like we've really hit pay dirt, doesn't it? Should I be the first to welcome you to your new home? Tell you what — let's put it on paper and just see how it looks."

Or: "Looks like we've come pretty close, doesn't it? Let me just ask you a favor. Will you be sure to invite me over for your housewarming party?" Keep it light, laugh, and say whatever you have chosen to say in a relaxed, joking way.

At this point, you may encounter further hesitation in the form of the same objection surfacing again, or a new objection. If there's a new objection, you know what to do. Acknowledge it and give an empathetic phrase. If it's the same objection, you must deal with it, but only after you have isolated it as being the only problem.

For example: "Other than (their objection), is there anything else that is concerning you?" *Listen attentively, and then ask,* "What else besides that?"

If there is an objection regarding the property itself, acknowledge it without dwelling on it, then give a neutral, empathetic phrase such as, "I can sure appreciate how you feel."

Then use some probing questions. "Other than X, is there anything else that would keep this home from meeting your needs?"

Do not say: "Other than X, what would keep you from making a decision?" This emphasizes the wrong target. This places the emphasis on the dread of decision making instead of the remedy to a problem. One adds to the stress and pressure by alluding to what most people hate to do — make a decision — and the other relieves some stress and pressure by focusing on the solution.

Let the prospects reiterate all of their concerns. But don't try to answer them. If you start trying to answer each one as it comes, you will find yourself in a "skeet-shooting" predicament. As soon as you shoot one out of the sky and it disappears, here comes another! So, sit back, relax and let the concerns flow.

Don't interrupt. Just listen. Empathetically.

As Frank Bettger, author of *How I Raised Myself from Failure to Success in Selling,* states, "People have two reasons for doing anything — the real reason and the one that sounds good."

Usually, the first few objections that you hear are the ones that "sound good." The prospects are just not yet convinced that the value and benefits for them outweigh the value of their cash. Here again, that fear of making a wrong decision emerges.

The very last thing you want to be is combative or argumentative. Remember, you are not there to confront. You are there to comfort. Agree that maybe they are right. Maybe they should talk with their accountant, ask their lawyer, sell their home, think about it, or whatever. Then acknowledge that if these problems or concerns were solved, then they would be ready to proceed. Like this:

Sales Ace: "Jason, Ashley, if X was taken care of to your satisfaction, would you feel comfortable in moving forward with this home?"

Agree with them again that maybe they shouldn't until their problem is solved, but drop a seed from your "fear-of-loss pouch" into their minds. For example:

Sales Ace: "Well, it's your decision. Maybe you are right. Maybe you should not move on with it until you've asked your accountant's opinion. The only thing that concerns me is the value of this home and the way properties have been moving around here. But if it's gone, it's gone. Then I guess it just wasn't meant to be." (You get to say it before they do! Don't you just *love* it!?)

Then tell a true third-party story about another person you worked with who hesitated and lost out, maybe came back later and bought something else, but had to pay more for it.

Sales Ace: "I'd hate to see that happen to you folks. But I want you to do whatever you want to do. It's your decision. Tell you what — let's put together a sample agreement so you'll know how it looks on paper. Then you'll have it to take home with you."

If you meet with the objection again, relax, stay low and slow in your speech, and empathize with them. For example:

Sales Ace: "I can sure appreciate how you feel," or, "If I were in your situation, I would probably feel the same way."

Then make use of one of your answers to that objection, or an emotional close. Keep in mind that the process of closing must be like the waves of the sea. Just as they come in and go out, so must you, the sales ace, advance and retreat.

In fact, gradually moving the prospect to a buying decision by removing the objection could even be compared to beach erosion. The sand dune is the mental barrier or the main objection in the prospect's mind, holding him back from making a decision. The influx of the waves picks up sand from the dune and the outward flow carries the sand with it, gradually removing the dune.

As a sales ace, you have the same effect by using your "advancements" on the main objection. But what are the advancements? And when do you retreat?

ADVANCE AND RETREAT

The sales ace advances by the use of additional benefits of the property, good reasons for buying now, fear-of-loss statements, testimonials, written documentation of an earlier selling point, or any other form of encouragement to proceed with the purchase.

Then, like a wave, the ace must retreat with one of the following release phrases:

- "But it's your decision; it's totally up to you."
- "Do whatever you want to do; it's your decision."
- "But I don't want you to do it unless you feel comfortable with it."
- "Don't even consider it unless you are excited about it."

When you advance, you're planting additional seeds for thought. When you retreat, you are allowing some light to come in and help those seeds grow.

The retreating process is extremely important and must be handled in a sincere, yet nonchalant manner. This process involves backing away verbally or it may even mean backing away physically, shown by your posture or by your absence for a while to relieve some pressure. This gives the prospects room to make their decision. They need to feel that it is totally their decision.

If you place yourself in a *confronting* posture instead of a *comforting* one, you begin to develop an adversarial relationship. It's easy to come across in an argumentative way. The prospects feel you are trying to get them to change their minds. That is not your goal. Be aware that people do not want to change their minds! If they do, they have to admit that they were wrong the first time. They may fear losing face.

So what you want is not to change their minds but help them make a new decision based on additional information that you can provide.

Top sales ace Johnny Ussery has an interesting technique he uses to increase the prospect's fear of loss. This comes after he has done everything he can think of without turning the prospect off. He has them emotionally excited about one particular site, one home, that one-of-a-kind for them. But for some reason, he just can't get them to budge.

So he sits back and very sincerely says, "Well, folks, I've accepted the fact that you need more time, and that's fine. Naturally, it's your choice; however, as strong as the market is we need to take another fifteen minutes and pick out your second favorite choice of site. That way when we talk tomorrow or Wednesday, if this one is gone, at least we haven't wasted our time. We can always move to our second choice."

He really means this, because he has told story after story throughout the presentation about others who have hesitated and lost out. It's a good way to increase the fear of loss. It can't be stressed too much that this automatically accelerates that sense of urgency to buy. You need an attitude of "It makes no difference to me, it's up to you."

But before you say goodbye to these prospective buyers, you need to be sure that you have one of four possible commitments from them.

FOUR COMMITMENTS

1. Of course, the first and best is getting a fully-executed purchase agreement with a strong deposit.

2. The second-best commitment you can get is getting a reservation to put a property on hold for a specified period of time. The key is to create a reason to get back together. They must become emotionally attached to one particular property. Keep in mind that the first step to the big sale is the small sale, and dropping from the agreement to the reservation is the next-best thing.

3. If you can't get a sales commitment, and you can't get a reservation, then go for the appointment commitment. Try to get them to come back again and go over some things that were perhaps not covered this first time.

4. If you can't get the commitment for a return visit at a later date, then go for the callback commitment. Say, "Jason, Ashley, would you be offended if I give you a call in the next couple of days just to get your feelings about the other places you are seeing?" Find out how to reach them and then get on that phone and give them a call. Nothing beats that intense follow-up call after the first appointment.

No salesperson closes them all, but you will close the close ones if you close with empathetic compassion and a sincere belief that it is the prospect who will be the real loser if he or she doesn't decide.

I determine the atmosphere in which I abide by the attitude I adopt.
— T. L. Weaver

13

CALLING IN THE ARTILLERY TO OBLITERATE OBJECTIONS

One of the biggest problems most salespeople have surfaces when they receive an objection (to making a decision) from their prospect. How do we deal most effectively with this? Most salespeople cower when they hear their prospects procrastinate. Why? Because most salespeople have not spent the time to think through good ways to dissolve each objection and encourage the prospect to cross the buying threshold. Ask yourself the following:

- If your prospects have gotten their questions answered.
- If they feel excited about the community concept.
- If they have found the ideal property.
- If they can afford this dream home without it becoming a nightmare.
- If you believe in your heart that it is the best thing for them.
- If you believe that property values are going up and it will cost them to procrastinate.
- If you believe they will thank you a year from now if they do cross the threshold, and kick themselves if they do not, then you have a moral responsibility to sincerely counsel these people into their buying decision.

But how? Do not think of it so much as selling something to someone. Think of it as *counseling* people about doing what they should do. It is about making a wise decision, not just a right one. They must see you as a compassionate counselor now and not as a commission-crazed closer. For this closing technique to be effective, they must like you, believe you and trust you, and be emotionally involved with the community and a particular property.

Let me prepare you for what you are about to read. If I don't, some of you may react to it like a vampire to a cross. You may think, "No, I couldn't do that. That's just not me." Or you may think it sounds canned. But that's only because it's being read out of context and you haven't learned it like you know your own name and address. If you read lines out of a romantic love scene in a play, they may sound hokey, but in context, with high emotions being delivered by an expert actor, they sound quite natural.

Stop and think about it. How many actors write their own lines? How many singers sing their own songs? Some do, and you, too, should always be thinking so that you can creatively come up with answers to objections. What I am giving you is a good place to start building confidence so you will not be blown away by objections that you otherwise could overcome.

The primary idea in dealing with objections is to get the prospect's mind off the fearful decision-making process and onto the benefits they will enjoy by owning in your community. When dealing with fear, which is usually the emotion blocking the prospect from deciding (the fear of a making a wrong decision), we must *comfort,* not *confront.* These answers must be given in a laid back and sincere manner. They don't necessarily have to be memorized, but the better you know them the more confidence you will have in giving them. They shouldn't be so diluted that they lose the punch of their point.

Think about a circus for a minute. Probably the clown is the best tightrope walker in the entire circus. The clown is the one who has learned the act perfectly up on the high wire, and has then been able to ruffle it up and act like a nut up there without killing himself.

You are much the same way. Perfectly learn what you are planning to say, then "ruffle it up" to make it sound like you and not some canned speech.

One thing to keep in mind is that prospects may be emotionally stuck in this moment. This fear, or the problem of over-analyzing the situation, may be giving them "paralysis due to analysis." This is what could be keeping them from moving forward.

The best thing to do is to simplify the whole process: Help them step back and take a glance into the future at all the fun and enjoyment they're going to have by owning there. Why not give them the Crystal Ball Close....?

CRYSTAL BALL CLOSE

"It's only natural, Jason and Ashley, that you want to make sure that you are making a wise decision. It sure would come in handy if we could actually look into the future a little bit, wouldn't it? This may sound a little crazy to you, but go along with me on this one.

"Let's just imagine we are looking into a crystal ball and can actually see into the future. Let's assume you decide to buy this place, and we are looking a couple of years down the road. Let's say I bump into you then and say, 'Jason and Ashley, how in the world have you been? How do you like your place here at Eagle's Roost?' If you see yourself saying, 'It's been fantastic. In fact, for the last couple of years, we've accumulated all kinds of memories of good times, relaxation on the beach, numerous rounds of golf with new friends on these beautiful courses and we really are proud of what we have here. It's a pleasure to be able to share it with our friends and relatives. Besides that, we get a chance to enjoy using some of our hard-earned money by deducting our interest and actually saving some dollars that would otherwise go to the government for taxes.'

"Jason and Ashley, if you were looking back on it, and that was the way it actually turned out, do you think you would ever really regret making the decision to own your own place here at Eagle's Roost?" (Slowly shake your head at this point.) "You probably wouldn't, would you?

"Jason and Ashley, I encourage you both to go ahead and make your decision based on that being the outcome. Why don't we go ahead and get the process started?"

Or perhaps you have already concluded that the prospective buyers are not the crystal ball type. There are other resources in your arsenal.

The primary emotion that your prospect has to deal with is the fear of making the wrong decision or the fear of looking foolish. So how do you handle the fear? By comforting, not confronting.

Build up their confidence based on their past successes. Try the Right Decision Close.

THE RIGHT DECISION CLOSE

"Jason, Ashley, you may not have realized this, but you two are very rare individuals. Do you realize that the vast majority of the world can only dream about doing what you actually have an opportunity to do right here — owning your own beautiful place on an island (or a mountain or a lake) like this? Actually, I really admire and respect the fact that you are even in a position that you can do something like this. It just shows me that you've worked awfully hard all your life and made a lot of right decisions.

"Making a decision about owning property here will simply be just another in that long list of right decisions. Do you feel good about this home? Could you see yourselves really enjoying it and building a lot of great memories here? Great! Why don't we go ahead and make *one more* right decision that you can look back on by tying up this home for you?"

Remember, this is an emotional decision. The following counseling tools may help you, but only if they are said from your heart.

MAKING A LIFE

"Jason and Ashley, it's kind of like one of our owners said one time: 'I seem to spend so much time making a living that often I ignore making a life.' Many people are in that same boat today, aren't they? One of the reasons so many people buy property here at Fantasy Island is because it helps them to get their priorities in better order by putting their money into something that will be not only a good investment in the long run financially, but also a true investment into the quality and enjoyment of their lives.

"After all, life is so brief. What good does it do for a person to work himself to the point of a heart attack and not spend that money on improving his lifestyle? Can you see how owning a home on this beautiful island would not only give you some good tax advantages, but at the same time give you a great deal of personal enjoyment and real pride of ownership?"

And, after their response, you say, "Great, let's go ahead and get things started."

If not, you can always remind them of the memories they will create in their new home.

CHERISHED MEMORIES CLOSE

"Jason, did your folks have a vacation home when you were growing up?" (Assume he says no.) "Wouldn't it have been great if you could have enjoyed a place like this with your folks as you were growing up? I'll bet a lot of super memories could have been made, couldn't they? Wouldn't it be great to be able to provide something like this for your children and family to help them build some of those memories? Jason and Ashley, there really are some things that you can't put a price tag on, aren't there? Valuable family memories would certainly be one of them, wouldn't they?"

REAL ESTATE VERSUS STOCKS AND BONDS

"Jason and Ashley, do you do quite a bit of investing in the stock market?" (Assume they say yes). "One of our owners once said that he had never received very much real personal gratification or fulfillment from investing his money in the stock or bond market, limited partnerships, or apartments back home. All he ever got were a few dollars and a number of headaches.

"He just felt that as hard as he worked for his money, he deserved to have some of his money in a place that could give him not only some good financial rewards, but at the same time offer those personal rewards as well. He felt a place like this with everything it has to offer would fill that kind of need.

"After all, what good is money if we can't use it to increase the quality and enjoyment of our lives? Right? Why don't we go ahead and start increasing that quality right now?"

TAKE TIME TO LIVE

"You know, folks, I really enjoy observing different bumper stickers, don't you? One that really hit me simply said, 'Take time to live.' You know, that sounds so simple, but with the hectic pace that so many people keep today, taking time to live is much easier said than done, isn't it? I believe one of the reasons so many people get excited about investing their money into Fantasy Island is because they realize they are not just investing in *making a living*, but they are investing *in living*.

"After all, we've all heard of people who have sold their soul to the company store and pretty much put off living year after year until they woke up one day and realized there wasn't a lot of living left. It's like a client of mine said, 'If I'm going to work like crazy to afford something like this home that improves my life, it only makes sense for me to have it while there's still time to enjoy it.'

"Makes sense, huh? I guess it's kind of like Billy Graham said one time: 'I've never seen a hearse pulling a U-Haul yet!' Do you feel you'd be proud to own a home like this? Do you feel you would really enjoy creating some great times? Great, let's do it!"

PRACTICING RETIREMENT

Think of this as a way of helping people realize this can be a no-lose situation. "Jason, you and Ashley remind me an awful lot of another couple who picked up a homesite with retirement in mind. They felt it would be a good idea to start coming to Magic Mountain every year to see if they really enjoyed it here as much as they thought they would. They called it 'practicing their retirement.'

"They realized that by the time retirement comes some other place may appeal to them more, but if not, and if they still love Magic Mountain as much as they think they will, then they would not be moving to a strange place to retire. With their familiarity with it and the friends they would have made, it would be more like 'going home.'

"They felt that even if they *did* decide to retire someplace else, then at the worst they would have made a good financial investment. Either way, they won. Does that make sense to you? Is that about the way you folks feel, too? Great! Why don't we go ahead and get things started?"

A real key is also helping them understand that money is a small price to pay for all the value that they're going to get.

THE DISNEY TICKET CLOSE

Use this for overcoming price objections to a homesite or a home: "Jason, Ashley, let me ask you something. Have you ever taken your kids to Disney World? How much does one of those day-long tickets cost? Probably close to fifty dollars. Well, if you just took that ticket, that little piece of cardboard, how much would it really be worth?"

Jason: "Oh, maybe five cents."

Sales Ace: "That's probably about right, but that little ticket has much greater value than just a nickel because it opens the doors for a day filled full of fun, experiences, and memories, doesn't it? This place is very similar. You could cut the trees down and sell them for lumber. You could scoop up a few tons of dirt and sell it. But you probably would never get anywhere close to the two hundred and fifty thousand dollars.

"That's because the real value of this place is that it's like your ticket. It's what opens the door for you and your family to enjoy (list some of the amenities at this point) and build the memories that come with those experiences. Does that make sense to you?

"Besides, it's really hard to put a price tag on those kinds of life experiences, isn't it? Why don't we go ahead and get that ticket taken care of before someone breaks in line in front of you?"

THE BALANCE SHEET CLOSE

"You know something, Jason and Ashley? Decisions like these are never easy, are they? Some folks I've seen in the past have simply thought about it for a little while, got their feelings all wrapped up in it, and then ended up making an emotional decision that they later regretted. Some of them bought, some of them didn't. Would you like to try to avoid making an emotional decision which you may regret?

"A wise man I once heard of found a way to do this. When he found himself in a situation such as you are in today, he felt pretty much as you do about it. If it was the right thing, he wanted to be sure to go ahead and do it, but if it was the wrong thing, he wanted to be sure to avoid it. Isn't that about the way you feel, too?

"To be able to really sort out his feelings, he would take a sheet of plain paper and draw a line down the middle of the page." (Do this as you speak.) "On one side, he simply wrote 'yes' and under it he listed all the reasons to do something, and on the other side, he wrote 'no' and listed all the reasons against it. When he was through, he simply counted up the list, and his decision was pretty much made for him.

"That makes sense to me. Does it to you? Let's just try it with you and see what happens. Let's think of all the advantages for you in owning here at Fantasy Island. Let's think of all the disadvantages. Now let's count them. Well, a wise decision seems pretty obvious, doesn't it?"

Don't hesitate here more than a split second. Go right into the closing question. "Jason and Ashley, I bet you a year from now, you'll be looking back and thanking me for my help today. Let's go ahead and get things started for you. You'll be glad you did."

DEALING WITH SPECIFIC OBJECTIONS

Most of the time, objections are only smokescreens to avoid making a decision. The first time you hear an objection, you should ignore it. That's right. Don't try to answer it directly the first time because that simply glamorizes it. You simply acknowledge it, ignore it, and show more of the property to build more value. If the same objection surfaces again, then you must deal with it. Face it straight on without any hesitation and with an attitude of quiet, sincere confidence. Clients are going to reflect your body language and your attitude. Let's see if we can deal with a couple of the specific ones you hear quite often.

"It just costs too much." Use the old "reduce it to the ridiculous" close:

Sales Ace: "You know something, Jason, it seems like today almost everything does. Can you tell me how much too much you feel it is?"

Purchaser: "Probably fifty thousand dollars."

Sales Ace: "Fine. My thought here, Jason and Ashley, is that we should put this into proper perspective." Here, hand over your pocket calculator and say, "Let's just say that you owned this home. I believe you said you'd be financing it, isn't that right?"

Purchaser: "Yes."

Sales Ace: "OK, you need only ten thousand dollars more down. That costs about seven dollars per month for every one thousand dollars in mortgage, so multiply seven dollars times forty for your extra forty thousand dollars in the mortgage, and we get two hundred eighty dollars per month, don't we? Now, how about dividing that by thirty days, and see what we get."

Purchaser: "Around nine dollars."

Sales Ace: "Do you think that it's wise to let nine dollars per day cause you to settle for a home that's just adequate, rather than one that you're really excited about?"

Purchaser: "Well, I don't know."

Sales Ace: "I understand how you feel, Jason. One of our owners said to me when he was considering his purchase, 'Terry, the great thing about real estate is that every day I pay this extra nine dollars per day, I can get tax deductions from 95 percent of it, which is interest and at the same time the real estate is probably appreciating. So it really doesn't cost me anything.'

"You know, Ashley and Jason, it sure makes good sense to invest in real estate, doesn't it? This nine dollars after taxes is probably only about five dollars per day. And the main thing that excites me for you is that I sense this is the home you'd really enjoy, wouldn't you? Do you like the feel of it? Do you like the floor plan? Is it large enough? Do you see yourselves being happy here for years to come? Wouldn't it be a shame to miss getting what you really want?"

Purchaser: "Yes."

Sales Ace: "Fine. Would you promise me something? Would you promise to invite me over to your housewarming?" Keep it light with a smile and a chuckle.

Purchaser: "Sure, we will."

Sales Ace: "Great. Now, would you be taking title in only one of your names, or in both your names?"

"The price is just too high." Time for the Quality Close.

Sales Ace: "Jason and Ashley, our company had to make a choice between developing our property as cheaply as possible and selling it as a get-buy product that almost anyone could afford, or building quality into it for service, durability, and your long-lasting enjoyment.

"With this decision facing us, our company made a basic decision. We decided that it would be easier to explain price one time than it would be to apologize for lack of quality forever." (Slight pause.) "I'll bet you're glad we made that decision, aren't you? Why don't we go ahead and start taking a look at the paperwork, so you folks can start enjoying this quality?"

"I have to talk with my accountant, or my lawyer or...."

Sales Ace: "Jason and Ashley, it's kind of like a client of mine once said when asked if he felt he could get his accountant's permission on a piece of property he was looking at. He said, 'My accountant probably makes one hundred thousand dollars per year. I make considerably more than that. He is not paid to tell me what I can and cannot do. He is paid to tell me the best way to structure the things that I tell him I want to do.'

"You know, that really makes a lot of sense, doesn't it? Is owning this home something that you really want to do? Great! Let's do it!"

Or, try a light-hearted approach: "You know, Jason and Ashley, that reminds me of the story about these two guys who were up in a hot air balloon. The wind blew them above the clouds and they became totally disoriented. The balloon finally dropped below the clouds and they saw a man in his yard.

"They hollered down and said, 'Sir, where are we?'

"The man looked up and said, 'Why, you're in a hot-air balloon.'

"The wind shifted and took them up above the clouds. One guy looked at the other and said, 'That guy had to be an accountant, because what he said was 100 percent accurate and totally useless.' (Laugh.)

"Now, I'm not saying, Jason and Ashley, that the things your accountant tells you are totally useless because I am sure that he gives you wise counsel on anything that he is familiar with. When was the last time he was down here on Fantasy Island? You see, he's not familiar with this place and what it has to offer and the values down here. It would be kind of hard for him to give you good, sound advice.

"After all, you and your family are the ones who are really going to be enjoying this place, aren't you? Do you feel like you'll really take the time out of your schedule to come down and use it? Why don't we go ahead and take a look at the paperwork so you can start using it as soon as possible?"

When you hear objections like having to talk with the accountant, these are so vague that it is difficult to handle. You need to get the objection expressed in such a way that you can put a handle on it so that you can deal with it. Something like the following may be helpful:

Sales Ace: "So you feel like you need to talk with your accountant?"

Purchaser: "Yes, we always discuss our financial decisions such as this with him."

Sales Ace: "Let me see if I understand what you're saying. Are you saying that you need to discuss this with your accountant so that he can tell you if you can afford to own a home here, or would your accountant simply be telling you how to arrange this purchase in your portfolio go give you the best tax advantages?"

Purchaser: "He'll tell us if we can afford it."

Sales Ace: "Did you say that you'd probably finance your home?"

Purchaser: "Yes."

Sales Ace: "Well, I have some good news for you. The reason you won't need your accountant to tell you is that the lenders here loan money based on the Golden Rule"... (pause and smile)... "He who has the gold, makes the rule. In other words, if your finances don't fit their rules, they will not loan you their money. And based on the figures we've already talked about, the lender would surely feel confident that you would be able to afford it, wouldn't he?"

Or, assume the prospect says something like the following:

Purchaser: "He wouldn't tell us if we can afford it; he would just tell us how to arrange it for our taxes."

Sales Ace: "Do you have a pretty good accountant?"

Purchaser: "Sure."

Sales Ace: "Is he pretty efficient?"

Purchaser: "Yes."

Sales Ace: "Do you feel he could arrange it properly for your portfolio in the next three or four weeks?"

Purchaser: "Oh, yes."

Sales Ace: "Great! That won't cause us any problem today, then, because the decisions about how property should be titled or where it should be placed in your portfolio doesn't even have to be made until near closing, and it will be at least six weeks before we close. Does the home have the kind of view you are looking for? Does it have enough space for you? Can you see yourselves enjoying it with your family? Why don't we go ahead and proceed so that you can start enjoying it as soon as possible?"

Or, use this one for procrastination:

Purchaser: "We just need to think about it some more."

Sales Ace: "I'm glad. I want you to think about it. You know what though? I've learned there are two types of people who 'think about it.' The first type will tend to head back home and let all the concerns of life, fears of the unknown, timing, money, or whatever causes them to 'think' their way right out of doing something for themselves that they deserve, would enjoy, and be glad they did. The second type are the ones who clearly understand the opportunity, feel good about it, and head back home thinking about all the fun and plans for their future. They wonder who'll be the first friends they will invite down, when they will return to enjoy their place, etc.… those kinds of exciting thoughts. Question for you: which kind of thoughts would *you* rather carry back home with you?"

Or try this alternative for "needing to think about it":

Sales Ace: "That's fine, Jason and Ashley. Obviously, you wouldn't take your time thinking about it unless you were seriously interested in it, would you?"

Purchaser: "That's right."

Sales Ace: "Since you are that interested, may I assume that you will give it very careful consideration?"

Purchaser: "Oh, yes, we will."

Sales Ace: "Just to clarify my thinking, what is it that you want to think over?" (No pause here.) "Is it the location of this villa?"

Purchaser: "No, we like the location."

Sales Ace: "Is it the quality of the construction? Is it the size of the villa? Is it the architecture that you don't like?"

As you go through five or six of these things and none of them is the problem, then finish by saying, "Well, I give up. You've got to help me out. What is it that you really need to think about? Is it maybe the financial investment that's involved in owning this villa?" If this is the problem, then you need to focus specifically on the value of the villa's use versus the price that's being paid.

Or, how about this one:

Sales Ace: "I can sure appreciate that, Jason and Ashley. I know you want to make sure you're making the right decision for yourselves, don't you? Let me throw out something for you to think about.

"Imagine for a minute that you are sitting in a class, maybe even back in college. Didn't you say you went to UNC? Let's say the professor walks into a big lecture hall, flips the lights off, and shows you a film. You don't take notes because it's dark. Afterwards, he announces that he's going to give you a quiz on what you just saw and heard. It will count for half of your grade. He says you can take the quiz right then, or in a week. When would you probably take it?"

Purchaser: "Probably right then!"

Sales Ace: "Why?"

Purchaser: "Because it's fresh on my mind."

Sales Ace: "That's right, Jason. Now, I realize that buying a homesite here is a lot more important than a quiz in college, but the principle is really about the same. Isn't the best time to make a good decision on something when the facts are still fresh in your mind?

"Jason and Ashley, I want you to do this only if it's the right thing for you, and is what you really want to do. Let me ask you a question. What is it that appeals to you most about this homesite?"

Ask several other questions, ending with this final close question: "Why don't we just see how it looks on paper?"

SHOULD'VE/WOULD'VE CLOSE

Sales Ace: "A friend of mine told me his wife got sick and tired of hearing him say, 'I **should've** bought beach (lake, mountain) property ten years ago and I **would've** if I'd known this was going to happen. All of us have said that, haven't we? It doesn't take any real brains or special insight though to report the past, does it? But it *does* take insight and confidence to project into the future. Every day, 12,000 people turn 50 years old in the United States alone. And with 77 million of these Baby Boomers (who will be inheriting 10 trillion dollars) do you think five years from now, you'd be saying 'glad I did' versus 'should've/would've'? "

(Response)

Sales Ace: "Great, let's make that happen for you!"

THE INSURANCE CLOSE

As a final closing attempt to get the prospects to at least take some kind of action when they are determined to look at other areas, get them into a discussion about insurance.

"Jason, Ashley, do you have various kinds of insurance? What different kinds do you carry? Why do you carry all those different kinds of insurance?

"Protection against loss."

"Then let me ask you this. How do you really feel about this site overlooking the water?" (You must have narrowed it down to a unique property that he or she has become emotionally involved with.)

"Let me ask you another question. "How would you feel if you lost it? If someone else came in and bought it out from under you?"

If the prospects indicate that they would be somewhat disappointed, then you've got something to go on.

"How would you like to have some insurance against this possible loss, just like the other things you insure? Now I realize you want to go look around other places, and that's fine. Maybe you should. In order for you to do that and still protect yourselves against the loss of this site, why don't we just write it up in a reservation form with a one thousand dollar deposit that will pull it off the market for forty-eight hours?" (Or whatever your manager allows.)

"That will give you some additional time to get even more excited about us. How does that sound?"

Obviously, this should be your "last resort" close because of its lack of strength. Since the law in most states gives them usually seven days to rescind their decision anyway, what do we have to lose by getting them on paper? At least you're getting them to take some sort of action.

BECOMING A CREATIVE CLOSER

As good and as useful as all of the previous answers to objections are, nothing beats being creative and customizing a close for that specific customer who is on the very verge of buying. Doesn't it just drive you crazy when the people are so close and you can't come up with something to pull them over the edge?! There are two keys that can help you become better at this:

- Know as much good pertinent and personal information about your prospect as possible.
- Think in terms of analogies. How does buying this property relate to something else that is important to them?

Sales Ace Rocky Stellings from Kiawah Island told me an excellent example of this. He was working with a lady who was a big Cleveland Indians fan. They had skyboxes and the whole deal. He was showing her a particular housing product in which there was only one piece of property left.

She happened to tell him that she had looked at a product very similar to that several years ago in another community, but that her accountant had talked her out of it. She said that several months before that she had seen a very similar product in another competing community, but she just couldn't decide how it was going to turn out when it was completed.

Being the quick thinker that Rocky is, he related her situation directly to her love of baseball. He looked her straight in the eye and said, "It sounds to me like you're zero and two and I'm not going to throw any balls. If you don't swing at this next one, you're out!"

She looked at him, and then smiled and said, "Good point."

Before Rocky could even sit down in his office, she came up to the door and said, "We'll take it!" That was a four hundred twenty-five thousand dollar sale. In the last two years she has bought two oceanfront homesites that were worth over $1.2 million each.

Rocky also told me about the importance of using this information as well as what you learn in other places. Rocky attended an ACES Academy in 1998. He was listening to Jim Chaffin, who was past president of Urban Land Institute and Spring Island Company tell about the 77 million Baby Boomers coming of age and rushing across the hills with their pockets full of money and looking for high quality real estate.

Rocky had a prospect on the verge of buying a $2.2 million oceanfront site, but he was unable to pull him across that buying line. After listening to Jim, Rocky went right to the telephone and called the gentleman. He told him exactly what he had just learned, and the prospect said, "That makes sense to me. Let's go ahead and do it!"

That was in January of 1998. Eight months later, that site was worth $2.9 million.

Regardless of how much money people have and how much of it they may have spent in the past, they need you to navigate them emotionally through the fearful, troubled waters of decision-making. A creative-analogy closing is one of the most powerful navigation tools you can use. Plus, you need a good variety of closes in your repertoire. The behavioral psychologist Abraham Maslow once stated, "If all you have is a hammer, every problem looks like a nail."

PRACTICE, PRACTICE, PRACTICE

To effectively use these various closes, you must practice. You won't use all of them. Pick out the ones you feel comfortable with. You need to learn them so well that you can practically repeat them without even thinking. You need to own them. You may want to re-word some of them to make them sound more like your own words.

Prepare yourself and learn what you're going to say in such a way that you can say it naturally. How are great actors able to perform, saying lines they have not written? Still, they can completely captivate the audience by what they are saying.

It's sort of like the cello player who was supposed to be playing at a certain time in Carnegie Hall. He became totally disoriented in the big city and frantically walked up to a wino on the street exclaiming, "How do I get to Carnegie Hall?"

The wino looked him straight in the eye and said emphatically, "Practice! Practice! Practice!"

In his book, *New Home Sales,* David Stone says it masterfully: "The art of sales is learned the hard way by acquiring and practicing the basic skills every day. Skill comes when habit frees you from the need to concern yourself with the mechanics of your actions."

So, practice your skills! Decide to become a sales ace, a master!

I haven't been able to find the name of the author of the following poem, but it is indeed a classic. It sums up the life of many people I have known, especially one person that I have known quite well: me! I've known a number of people who have also used this poem effectively as a final closing tool.

Reluctant Buyer's Lament

I hesitate to make a list
Of all the countless deals I've missed;
Bonanzas that were in my grip —
I watched them through my fingers slip;
The windfalls which I should have bought
Were lost because I over thought;
I thought of this, I thought of that,
I could have sworn I smelled a rat,
And while I thought things over twice,
Another grabbed them at the price.
It seems I always hesitate,
Then make my mind up much too late.
A very cautious man am I
And that is why I never buy.
I chose to think and as I thought,
They bought the deals I should have bought.
The golden chances I had then,
Are lost and will not come again.

Today I cannot be enticed
For everything's so overpriced.
The deals of yesteryears are dead;

The market's soft — and so's my head!
At times a teardrop drowns my eye
For deals I had, but did not buy;
And now life's saddest words I pen —
IF ONLY I'D DECIDED THEN !!!

One of the best definitions of a salesperson I've ever heard is the following:

A professional salesperson is one who knows what to do and what to say, and how to do it and how to say it under every conceivable situation.
— The late William Maxwell, head of sales for Thomas A. Edison Electric, Inc.

THE FINE ART OF FOLLOW-UP AND FOLLOW-THROUGH

The follow up is one of the most important things you can learn to do to become great in this business.

When I was selling real estate on Hilton Head Island, South Carolina, the typical follow up system was the old index card files. The prospect's name was written on an index card and was placed either in the thirty-, sixty-, or ninety-day "tickler" file. I am sure it was quite a good method, however, I found that I never seemed to have the discipline or the organizational skills to master this system. Over the years I have found a lot of people who are just like me.

With today's computers and reasonably priced software packages such as Act!, BrightDoor, WinSales, Focus3, and Top Producer, there is absolutely no excuse to not have a thorough follow-up system.

One of the first follow ups you need to do with your prospect is just after you have accepted the fact that he or she is not going to buy at that moment. This contact may be in person just before they leave, or it could be over the phone just after they get home. At any rate, the purpose of it is to get referrals. Some possible phrases you may like to use are:

"Well, Jason and Ashley, I've accepted the fact that we're not going to be able to get you a place here this trip, but I do believe that you are sincerely interested, aren't you?"

"We sure are."

"Would you like me to keep in touch and keep you posted on what's happening so that when the timing is right for you we can find you that right place here in our community?"

"Yes, we sure would."

"I'll be glad to. By the way, would you be willing to help me out? I've learned that the best way to find the right kind of people for _____ (your community) is through people who already understand and appreciate it. I am talking about people like you. Could you name three people you know who would appreciate an invitation to learn about _____ (your community)? I'll give them a quick call and just invite them to come and take a look at us. You can be assured that they'll be treated with the same degree of respect and professionalism that you have been."

After they have given you the names and numbers, say, "Would you do me another favor? If you happen to bump into any of these folks, you may want to let them know that I'll be giving them a call just to invite them to learn more about our community and offer my services to them. I'd appreciate that."

Keep in mind that one of the reasons this type of approach is so effective in getting referral names is that the prospect often feels a little guilty that they have taken so much of your time and still haven't bought anything. Why not capitalize on that guilt of theirs so that at least you can walk away with some kind of accomplishment?

One of your first follow-up calls back to a good prospect should let him know that you will continue to keep in touch. In the conversation, you may want to weave in something like this:

"Well, Jason, I want you to know that I'm interested in you and your needs, and I'll be following up with you until you buy or until you are no longer interested in us. Does that sound fair? Now, Jason, I'm going to depend on you to tell me if your interest ever ends. All right?"

This way he or she will not be surprised to hear from you on a regular basis.

PURPOSE OF FOLLOW UP

In my youth I always enjoyed watching the old trains come by my grandma's house. Those huge engines were powered by heat, and probably steam. When they wanted to increase the speed, they simply threw in more coal, which would raise the heat to create more pressure in the boiler and send more energy to the engine.

That's sort of the same thing you have to do with your prospect. If the prospect leaves emotionally attached to a certain property, which hopefully they will be, then you must add more fuel as soon as possible to build more pressure — not from you, but from the internal pressure they apply to themselves. It's that internal pressure that will get them to take action.

For an "A" prospect, the sooner the follow-up, the better. Jerry Starr, a sales ace for Lake Toxaway, a beautiful community in the mountains of North Carolina, was telling me about a couple from Tennessee he had worked with for most of the day. They finally became emotionally locked in on a beautiful two-acre homesite covered in trees with a wide rushing mountain stream and a forty-foot waterfall. Remember the *Reluctant Buyer's Lament?* Well, in this case, the lamenting buyer was me!

Anyway, the people loved it, but the problem in their minds was that the site was rather steep. They had trouble visualizing how they could actually place their home on it. They just didn't have enough courage to leap across that buying chasm and so they left without owning it. Jerry knew they were "A" prospects.

Immediately Jerry put his architectural drafting skills to work and drew a nice-looking elevation of a home on the same slope as that homesite. He colored it in and sent it to them by overnight mail so they would get it the next day after they had arrived home.

The next day, he took his video camera and shot other houses around the neighborhood to remind them about their neighbors, to zoom in on homes that had been built on similarly sloped sites, and to explain how they were built. Then he went to their site and shot the trees, the view, the stream, and the waterfall. He even taped the sounds to let them listen to it for a while. He got a large thermometer and leaned it up against a tree. He then zoomed in on it as he was talking with them about the 95-degree heat in Tennessee that week. The thermometer on the video showed a cool 82 degrees.

While the camera was running he set the thermometer against a rock in the stream. It registered 65 degrees. He described how they would feel sitting on their deck looking at their own personal waterfall and feeling the cool breeze from their very own mountain stream.

Then he sent the video by overnight mail.

Did they buy? The day after it arrived, they called Jerry and said, "You dog, you! We'll take it!" Do you think they're glad they did? They'd better be. They got my site!

The key here is to learn to focus on being creative versus just competitive. God gave us good minds to use. Some people use these cranial spaces as warehouses simply to store information. Others, the ones who really get on in this life, are the ones who use them as manufacturing plants to create ideas!

John Pinter, a top sales ace who sold property at Winding River near Southport, North Carolina, has learned his lessons well about being a "manufacturing plant of ideas." One of his prospects was a fine couple from the Northeast who loved the community and found their special site but couldn't make the decision to buy.

As soon as they left, John shot a personalized video of their site, the view, the surrounding homes, the clubhouse, etc., and sent it overnight it to them. The next day, knowing they were avid nature lovers, he bought beautiful books about the birds and animals of the local area. Then he sent those overnight. He said these folks said they "couldn't believe a salesman would take the time" to do that for them.

He knew from their tone on the phone that they were really close. He told them to relax and not worry about it. At around sundown he took his digital camera out and made photos of "their" sunset and e-mailed it to them. He called and told them to go online and see what their sunset looked like at that moment. They did. They bought a two hundred and seventy-five thousand dollar homesite.

HANG IN THERE!

I'm not saying that you never give up on a prospect, but that's not the problem with most salespeople. They give up way too soon. Situations change over time. Don't forget that according to economists at Cornell University, over the next three decades the Baby Boomers will inherit over ten trillion dollars. That's a lot of money!

To put it another way, a year or two can literally convert a "B" prospect into an "A." But you have to be in front of him or her if they are going to think of you and your place when the timing is right! That's one of the most important keys to successful marketing. *When the prospect is ready to buy, be in his mind.*

The following are some ideas just to help you get started thinking about how to follow up with your prospects:

- A phone call to them the day they are supposed to arrive back home from their visit with you just to check in and see if they made it back safely.
- If they are "A" prospects, a phone call from you every two weeks for the first two months and every month thereafter just to "update" them on what's happening. After three months, if they have still not bought, you may consider re-classifying them as "B" prospects.
- If they are "B" prospects, call them every six weeks to touch base and have some good news to share and some additional information that applies directly to their points of interest. If they are "C" prospects, call every six months just to check in and determine their interest level. These people can also be called by a sales assistant, if you happen to have one. You want to focus most of your energy and time on following up with the "A" list and the "B" list.
- They should receive a newsletter from you at least every other month. Your newsletter. Not the company's — yours. It doesn't have to be fancy. It just needs to be neat and present a good image. It doesn't have to be lengthy, maybe just the front and back of one page. It needs to contain some real estate news, what sold in the community, appreciation to various owners who have sent you referrals, welcome to the newest owners who have purchased from you, plus your "best buys." You may decide to share this responsibility with one of your fellow team members. It's been said correctly that "Many hands make light of a heavy task."
- If you happen to have a good relationship with some of your owners who are from the same towns that some of your "A" prospects are from, you may ask these owners to give the prospects a call, just to introduce themselves and offer to answer any questions they may have about your community. In other words, let them help you sell from a second party point of view. You may want to explain your intentions to your prospects.
- Notify your prospects and invite them to attend any off-site parties or presentations you may be having that take place near their town.
- The most important thing to remember is that this business is a contact sport! Persistence pays off, so be creative and disciplined in keeping your name, voice, face, and community in front of your best prospects.

FOLLOW THROUGH

As any knowledgeable athlete will tell you, when it comes to sports, it all depends on the follow through. It's the same thing in real estate. Unfortunately, failure to follow through is one of the biggest weaknesses for many in our industry.

In the world of real estate, a follow up is what you do for a prospect who still hasn't bought, and a follow through is what you do for a person who has already bought in order to solidify a strong relationship. Plus, you can reap numerous referrals and repeat business as a result of your follow through.

At the beginning of the book I asked you if you saw yourself as a professional real estate salesperson. Did you answer yes?

Stop it! You should now see yourself as a professional business person committed to building a successful real estate practice. The only way to do this is with excellent follow through with your customers after the sale.

Getting an agreement executed and closed is only the beginning. It only gives you permission to prove to the customers that you care more about them and their satisfaction than the commission that you collected. Doing this is the best way in the world to distinguish yourself from practically every other real estate salesperson they have ever encountered.

The only way you are going to build a successful real estate practice is through referrals, and only way you are going to get a lot of good referrals is by providing follow through service to your owners. This service attitude must begin immediately following their commitment to purchase.

The sooner you accept that only thing you really have to offer is service, the better off you will be and the more successful your life will become. Successful sales are a result of unselfish service. You need to see yourself as a servant. View serving as a privilege and not as an obligation.

One of the main ways you can distinguish yourself from others in the industry is by the degree of service that you offer during and after the sale. As any golf, tennis, or baseball coach will tell you, it's the follow through that counts! Follow through is what takes place after that buying decision is made.

There are only so many hours in the day. You can only handle so many walk-ins, and you can get your closing percentage just so high. The only way to dramatically increase your income and decrease the energy and time output is to focus on working referrals. You will close five times more referrals than first time walk-ins or appointments. A referral is in a much more receptive state when they meet you because they have at least been pre-sold on you. That is a big step in the right direction!

What really constitutes service in our business? Listening closely to the prospect's needs? Selling your community with enthusiasm? Finding the right property that best suits the prospect? Getting it closed smoothly? Giving a "welcome to our community" gift?

All of this is a part of service, but it goes much deeper than that. It's going the extra mile. It's doing the unexpected. Here's a good definition for you to memorize about service: *Service is the unexpected extra provided by you after the customer has received everything he or she expected from you.*

Jim Wedgeworth, the number one Realtor in South Carolina for more than sixteen years, couldn't agree more. He's been involved in more than 2,500 residential real estate transactions in the last 20+ years since he started in the business. He still keeps his "Top One Hundred" list of his absolute best clients who send him the most referrals.

Jim works exclusively on a referral basis and has done so since his second year in the business. That's absolutely incredible in our industry! In fact, it's unheard of! He decided after his first year that he was not going to do business the way he saw everyone else trying to do it by just waiting around for walk-ins.

He told me years ago: "I don't take walk-ins. I don't like walk-ins. They take up too much of my time. It's too much like selling copy machines to purchasing agents. You might get some good prospects, but you sure have to go through a lot of them to find the good ones."

He decided that he would build his business. He was going to service his customers in such a way that would cause them to want to send him referrals and help him build an organization that would support him and his family. He realized that it was the little things, going the extra mile, that would make the difference in the relationship that he would develop with his customers. He understands the importance of creating that personal loyalty with your customer through personal service.

Jim picks several each day from his top one hundred and asks himself what he can do in that month that would be special for them .

Several months ago Jim was riding through Sea Pines Plantation and happened to notice that the basketball net at the home of one of his "Top One Hundred" was hanging by one string. Knowing that his customer had two sons who played basketball, Jim phoned a student at the Christian Academy and asked him how much he would charge to replace that net within the next two days. He told them to "go ahead and fix it but make sure it's up by tomorrow afternoon."

A couple of days later the clients called and said, "Jim, do you know anything about this new basketball net?"

"Yea, I guess I do," Jim admitted.

The client said, "I knew it! I knew it was you!"

Several years ago a big snowstorm hit the Southeast and dumped about a foot of snow on Hilton Head Island. This was extremely unusual. While most people were scurrying to get to their homes, Jim went right to the drug store and bought up all the 35 mm rolls of film that they had. He rode slowly all over the island taking pictures of each of his clients' homes, home sites, and condominiums.

He took them to the one-hour film developer, collected the pictures, and took them home. While he was sitting in front of the fire with his family, he wrote Post-It-Notes on each picture: "Thought you'd like to see how your home looks with all this snow on it! Come on down and see me!"

Jim said he got more response from that picture effort than any mailing he'd ever done! Why? It's simple! It was personal. They knew that he had taken the time to do something over and above the call of duty. He had done the unexpected.

It's the little things that count. Spend as much energy on being creative as being competitive. In fact, more. It must work. It certainly has for Jim and it will for *you*.

Several years ago I asked Jim what made the difference in him that made him thrive while so many others were simply surviving.

What he told me was simple yet so profound: "Telephoning! Everyone sends out all this mass mail and waits for calls to come in or for someone to send back a business reply card, but no one picks up the phone to call owners or past prospects!"

"You don't have to try to sell them anything or try to get a listing. Just simply keep in close touch to see how their business is going, to keep up to date on their family, their health, and their holidays. Most people in our business think that their company owes them something. The company doesn't owe you a dime. They give us the opportunity and it just boils down to taking advantage of it by picking up the phone and calling somebody!"

How true, Jim! But it's those simple truths that seem to be most often overlooked.

In a sales transaction, from the time the decision is made until the closing, it's not unusual for a snag or two to appear. If that relationship is intact between you and the purchaser because of the service you have provided, then the vast majority of the time you will be able to sail right through that troubled water. Service is the oil that keeps the sales relationship lubricated and running smoothly. So check your service attitude. Is it a quart or two low? Been thinking too much about yourself and your own financial needs?

Your clients and prospects don't give a hoot about your mortgage payment or your future plans. They care only about their needs, desires, and happiness. How can you tell if you have been building the proper foundation? Simple. Look back at your sales over the last twelve months. If you've been in one community for three years, then at least 25 percent of your sales that third year should be from referrals. By the fifth year you should be having at least 50 percent of your sales from referrals.

If not, go back and check that dipstick. Sounds like you could be a little low and it is time to pull in for *service!*

FOLLOW THROUGH — NOW!

If you have been in our industry any length of time, you probably realize that the prospects who are the easiest to close and make the quickest decisions are often the first ones to back out. Their emotions go up like a rocket and come down like a rock. Don't assume anyone will stay hot and sold on their decision unless you keep that heat up.

Charlie Reed, a top sales ace on Hilton Head Island, once told me: "My goal is to solidify that bond with them after they have signed. The relationship is essential and keeping in close contact helps that to build. There will probably be some sort of problems arising between the time of signing and the time of closing, and the stronger my relationship with them, the easier it is to overcome the problem and keep the sale together."

Your people are most likely going to have doubts, so the best thing to do is prepare them for their next emotional onslaught while they are still in a reasonably logical state of mind. It is a big mistake if you do not spend at least twenty minutes with them just after they have approved the agreement. That is, of course, if they are with you in person. In a relaxed setting, discuss the following points with them:

- Your excitement for them and their future in your community.
- How it's going to be great to have them as a part of the community and how they will easily make friends there.

Because you have covered a lot of information they will probably forget some of the points in the next day or so that gave them the confidence to make this decision. Take your pad and with their assistance, jot down the reasons why they decided to get involved with you. Let them know that when and if they have any concerns and questions about their decision (which would be completely normal) to just look over this list and remind themselves of why they made that particular choice. Give them your phone numbers and let them know they can call you with any questions they have.

Often their concerns that surfaced during the sales process will pop up in a magnified form after the commitment has been made. Rarely do the prospects keep these concerns to themselves. They usually share them with their friends and colleagues who usually are quite ignorant of the situation but are free with their counsel and advice. Many times your new buyers are getting emotionally attacked so you had better make sure they have you as their "white knight" to ride in on a regular basis to save the day by building up their confidence in the decision they made.

If the buyers are with you, as soon as they have filled out their paperwork go out and take a photograph of them in front of their property. With the new digital cameras, this is easy. If they are not physically with you, go take a picture or a video (even better) of their purchase and get it in the mail to them as soon as possible.

Send a nice plant or flowers to their home just after they get there including a nice note that congratulates them on becoming a part of the Eagle Roost family!

If they are still nearby, have them meet you the next day to go over any additional information that you may have intentionally held back for follow through. It could be to get some information regarding builders, architects. It would be even better, if the timing is right, if they can actually meet with a couple of these people to get their thinking projected into the future. If they are purchasing a home, setting up a meeting with an interior decorator might be in order. Just keep their thinking occupied with positive activities and dreams of their future.

A handwritten note of appreciation from you is an absolute must. Let them know that you appreciate the confidence that they have placed in you, and that you look forward to earning their trust even more. Tell them that you hope they will feel comfortable sending their friends to you.

Manage their expectations. If it's a new home or an uncompleted condominium, prepare them for any possible delays or problems that could arise. Let them know that you are committed to helping them work toward a very smooth closing, so that they can start enjoying their home. Make a practice of under-promising and over-delivering. You will create happier and more satisfied customers. If there are going to be any surprises, make sure they are good ones.

Be a good sounding board. Realize that they occasionally need time to vent any concerns that they may have. Be a good listener and assure them that you care and will help them in any way possible.

Keep the additional information flowing to them regarding any articles about your community, the builder (positive ones), new collateral pieces, and special activities in the town or community. Everything they get from you needs to whisper softly to them, "You made a wise decision."

Ask for the names of friends and acquaintances who they feel might enjoy learning about your community. There is strength in numbers. It would be comforting to them to have friends who get excited about this community.

A nice housewarming gift is definitely in order. Deliver it personally and spend some time chatting with them. You may even decide to throw a party at the club for twenty or so of their closest surrounding neighbors. The theme would be something like "Come and welcome your newest neighbor!"

If the home is under construction and the buyers are out of town, regular photos or video updates of the building in progress would be a very good idea. Don't be like me, though! I was building a new home several years ago and decided to take a photograph of the front elevation and the rear elevation from the same spots every week... from site clearing, to foundation, to framing, roofing. Finally, I realized my camera was on picture number thirty-eight.

Panic gripped my throat as I hid in my closet and reluctantly opened up my camera to check it. Yep! No film! Did I feel like an idiot, or what?! Tillie didn't let me live that one down for quite some time.

You may even want to put these photographs into an album and when you've collected ten or twelve shots, send those to them and then update the shots every couple of weeks. Of course email makes it easier. It's that added service that makes the difference!

You can come up with many more ways to follow through. Just take three of your owners each day and ask, "What's something special I can do for them today that would be totally unexpected?"

If you expect them to do something for you like helping you build your business with referrals, then you must do something for them first. Have fun serving your way to the top!

The lower you bow in service to others, the higher the value they place on you.
— T. L. Weaver

AN UNSTOPPABLE POWER TO KEEP YOU MOTIVATED

You have had a chance to share in a great deal of knowledge from many sources in this book. But how do you stay motivated long enough to master these necessary skills?

How do you fight off the demons of discouragement that seem to lurk around every corner and turn in the road?

How is it possible, after years as an average producer taxiing down the real estate runway, to make your production and income take off? These are fair questions that deserve answers.

Am I saying that if you learn and use these past lessons, step by step, that you will automatically become a super ace in real estate sales? No. Not at all.

"But," you say, "if these are the correct steps, then logic tells me that if I follow them, I should, indeed, arrive."

That's true enough, as far as it goes; however, even though you will become much more productive, truly outstanding accomplishments are never achieved through logic. They are achieved by people who possess a powerful ability to maintain a high level of emotionally focused motivation through defeat after defeat until the task is achieved.

UNTAPPED POWER

The value of courage, determination, and perseverance has rarely been illustrated more convincingly than in the life story of this man:

Event	Age
Failed in business	22
Ran for legislature (defeated)	23
Again failed in business	24
Elected to legislature	25
Sweetheart died	26
Had a nervous breakdown	27
Defeated for Speaker	29
Defeated for Elector	31
Defeated for Congress	34
Elected to Congress	37
Defeated for Congress	39
Defeated for Senate	46
Defeated for Vice President	47
Defeated for Senate	49
Elected President of the United States	51

That's Abraham Lincoln! What an amazing example of persistence!

But how is this undaunted effort developed? Where do you find this power of motivation?

I am sure all of us have had days when we feel like our motivation tank has sprung a leak. In fact, have you ever had a day when you could hardly make yourself do what needed to be done? You pick up the phone and make those prospecting calls and it feels like you're picking up an anvil? You're having a meeting with new prospects and it feels like you're going for a root canal?

Yeah, me too! But the real question is: Why does this happen? Why do we have days when we're so excited about our work that we're like high-strung racehorses just waiting for the gate to open, and other days when we feel more like old nags pulling plows?

WHAT KEEPS YOU MOTIVATED?

I have experienced spurts of focused inspiration, but I had never really heard the secret of perpetual motivation put into words until several years ago. I had just completed a sales training seminar for a very successful builder in the Midwest. I got home late on a Friday night and early the next morning I received a phone call from him.

"Terry," he said, "I have one question for you. How do you keep yourself motivated?"

I said, "Chuck, that's a mighty good question, one that no one has ever asked me before. It deserves some thought … so I'll get back with you when I discover the answer myself."

A week later, I was in Charlotte, North Carolina, listening to a luncheon speaker. She was talking about the influence her dad had had in her life, and that one of the things he taught her was the secret to perpetual motivation. Naturally my ears perked up. Then she shared with us a statement that she had learned from her father. I have adopted it for myself and have taught it to many others. It is simple, yet profound: **Perpetual motivation and enthusiasm are the end result of a deeply-rooted purpose.** The deeper your purpose the high your motivation. It is the secret of staying motivated. It is the secret of staying motivated. Yes, I told you it was simple, but the most profound truths in life are simple.

Most people go through life missing a power that could transform their lives from a mere existence of mediocrity to a life filled with motivated meaningfulness. This power is available to everyone. It is *the power of purpose.*

Everyone who has ever achieved a high degree of success in anything has used this power. This same truth has started emerging for me in other areas, too.

Napoleon Hill spent twenty years of his life studying what made some people successful and what contributed to others' failures. In his best-selling book *Think and Grow Rich* he lists 31 reasons for why people fail at what they attempt. It was his opinion that the number one reason for failure that was controllable by the individuals was that they had "no well-defined purpose, no inner goal."

Your purpose is like your vision. It is the fuel that energizes you to accomplish your mission. It is the magnet that draws you and drives you to pay a price that most people are not willing to pay. It's what magnifies your motivation to a greater size than your fears.

Helen Keller was once asked, "Is there anything you can think of worse than being blind?"

After thinking for a while, she signed and said, "Yes, having eyes that can see, but having no vision."

An interesting story is told of the late great businessman, J. C. Penney. In his eighties, he was walking through one of his stores with an entourage of reporters around him.

One of them asked him, "Mr. Penney, it looks like your health is doing well. How is your eyesight?"

Mr. Penney looked at him and said, "Young man, my eyesight is not as good as it once was, but my vision has never been clearer!"

How many real estate salespeople have the ability to physically see what needs to be done and what the rewards of financial freedom could be, but have not developed that well-defined inner vision that fuels their motivation?

Several years ago I spoke with a Realtor friend of mine named Adele. She shared something quite interesting with me. She was experiencing her very best year ever in the tough real estate market of Florida. She told me that she had always had trouble getting on the telephone, but she said that making the phone calls this year, staying the extra hours, and truly being more enthusiastic had never been easier. I asked her why.

She said, "Terry, I've never been married, and my dad has always been concerned about my being able to support myself. I know it sounds silly, but he is of the old school. He discovered at the end of last year that he had terminal cancer, and so I made up my mind in January that this year was going to be for him. I was going to relieve his mind and prove to him once and for all that he never needed to worry about my future again."

That year, she had created something that most people lack, the power of purpose. If you lack purpose, then you will lack motivation, enthusiasm, and discipline. There's no doubt about it.

Just as those giant jet engines provide thrust to overcome drag and gravity and lift tons of steel gracefully into the sky, likewise purpose provides us with the thrust that overcomes the drag of work and the gravity that tries to hold us down.

What if you had a real fear of heights? Let's say someone offered you five thousand dollars to walk thirty feet out on an eighteen-inch ledge that was ten stories up in the air. Would you do it? Me neither!

Now change the situation. Let's say you have a one-year-old child who is really in the crawling stage. You're staying in a hotel and you're on the tenth floor. Not realizing the maid has left a window open, you walk into the bathroom and leave your child in the middle of the floor. You step out of the bathroom, and the baby's gone. You frantically look under the bed, behind the desk, and then you see the window that's open. Fear grips you like a vise as you reluctantly go over and look out. To your left, moving right along the eighteen-inch-wide ledge, is that crawling baby of yours.

Now tell me: How long would it take you to scoot out on that ledge now and attempt a rescue? What changed? It's simple. Your purpose changed. You see, the deeper your purpose, the higher your motivation and the less significant your fears. It's almost like a seesaw, isn't it?

This truth regarding the power of purpose and vision is nothing new. It was written at least 3500 years ago in Proverbs 29:18: "Without a vision, the people will perish."

What is true for the rest of the human race is also true for those who sell real estate. Without a vision, without a purpose, real estate people perish also. It happens all the time. People who have a deeply rooted purpose do not lack motivation or discipline. Sure, they may experience fear of failure like everyone else, but their purpose is strong enough to help them overcome that fear.

People who lack a well-defined purpose in their lives often suffer from low self-esteem. They have no drive, no burning desire to achieve, no striving for excellence, no passion to produce. They have trouble getting up in the mornings and putting in the extra effort that is so essential for success. They confuse activity with results. Remember, people who succeed are motivated by pleasing results. Those who do not are simply motivated by pleasing activities.

"But Terry," you may be thinking, "are you not talking about my goals?" Yes and no. Yes, the purpose is an integral part of your goal setting. But we need to spend some time analyzing goals so that you can truly understand how goals should be set in relation to your purpose.

Status quo. Here's another perspective. You are a SUCCESS. You have arrived at some milestone. Now what?

Remember those True/False tests we had back in school? Did you like them? Me either. But here is one worthy of your attention:

If I keep on doing the same things I've been doing in the same way I've been doing them, I'll keep on getting the same results I've been getting.

A. True   B. False

Sounds true, doesn't it? But it is false. Why? There is one key word that clarifies why it is not so. The word is **change.**

Our industry is undergoing incredible change. Just think how much change there is in communication, banking, medicine, computers (e-mail, the internet), and numerous other technologies.

The truth? *Whatever it took to get you here today is not enough to keep you here tomorrow.*

What do you call people or companies that do not embrace change? Often, the term is "obsolete" or "out of business." Remember the Sears catalog? Why don't we still receive that thick mass of pages in the mail? It went out of the catalog business in 1990. Maybe it had something to do with the fact that Sears did not even have a toll-free telephone number until 1987 and would not accept any charge card except the Sears card until 1989. By contrast, in 1990 Land's End did $640,000,000 in business! But Sears was smart. They bought Land's End.

In this world, *the status quo must go.* But for *you* to go, you must know where you're going. That's where goals come in.

> *The strength of your commitment is in direct proportion*
> *to the depth of your character.*
> — T. L. Weaver

16

PRODUCTIVE GOAL SETTING

It may help you to understand the proper way of setting goals by relating them to the three-legged milking stool.

The seat is the actual foundation of the stool. It can also be seen as the foundation of our goal setting. It should remind us of one of the biggest reasons why many people fail to accomplish their goals: they just use their seat too much!

Haven't you seen a lot of people who are always saying, "One of these days, I'm going to...." Then there's another group of people who say, "You know, if I had it to do over again, I'd...." The sad part about this is that these groups could easily represent the very same people separated only by time — about forty years of it.

If we don't set a specific time for when our goal challenge will begin, there is a good possibility that it won't. Have you ever heard yourself say, "One of these days I'm going to lose ten pounds, quit smoking, spend more time with my kids, and hit ten million dollars in sales"?

All of this sounds good and we all have great intentions, but when will we begin? My beautiful mom always used to say, "Terry, the road to hell is paved with good intentions."

The next question we have to ask ourselves is when our goal might be completed and have a target deadline. I believe it was the Alabama coach Bear Bryant who said, "I don't feel we ever lost a football game. We just ran out of time occasionally." That's a good attitude for belief and determination in winning, but each game does have its time restraints.

Why should we not impose on ourselves these same rules of time? Have you ever noticed how much more you accomplish when the pressure is on and you have to get it done? Have you also noticed the weird phenomenon of how a task will expand to the amount of time allotted for it? Why not get up off that seat and get on with that goal that is burning on the inside?

Let's use the analogy of the stool again. Each one of the legs must be intact or else you'll fall right on your ... good intentions. The same principle holds true for setting goals. Goals that really help direct and motivate someone to great accomplishment will have the following distinctive ingredients, or "support legs."

LEG ONE: WHAT I INTEND TO ACCOMPLISH.

This leg of your goal answers the *production* question. What kind of sales volume do you intend to produce by the year's end? What number of listings are you going to maintain? When asked by management what their goals are for the year, many salespeople pull a figure out of the sky, throw it down on a piece of paper, turn it in, and think they have set a goal for themselves. But they haven't.

You can plaster your year's volume goal all around the walls of your office and it will probably only frustrate you. It's like sitting down and looking at a twelve-ounce T-bone steak, and then trying to shove the whole thing in your mouth all at once. What could have brought delight brings disaster. You need to cut that steak up into one small chewable bite at a time so that you can enjoy it. The production goal is the same way.

You must learn to do what I was taught nearly thirty years ago when I sold books door to door. We were taught to break the major goal down into smaller bite-sized goals to *crystallize* our goals.

While I was selling books, after I had set my sales production goal for the week I would divide it by six and crystallize it as my daily goal. But to make the goal even more attainable and controllable, I would break the day down into three four-and-one-half hour parts. I also crystallized the production goal into those three parts. Then, rather than concerning myself with the large, long-term goal, I focused all my mental and physical energies on the attainment of the immediate goal at hand.

Have you crystallized your production goal for this year? Do you know exactly what you need to produce in terms of sales and listings required for this week in order to reach your long-term goal for the year?

If you are working in a seasonal market that has a lot more activity in certain times of the year, such as a resort area, you'll want to be sure and weight your production goal in favor of your stronger seasons.

An important point to remember here is to *not* stack your goals on top of each other. In other words, if you do not attain your goal for a particular week or month, do not stack it up on top of next week's or next month's goal. Simply forget it. Let the past die, and focus totally on your crystallized goal for the current period at hand.

Why is that important? Because if you start stacking goals on top of each other, they may become so large that they de-motivate you. There will be weeks, and maybe months, when you miss your goal, but there will also be other weeks or months that you will surpass it. Simply focus on the crystallized goal at hand and what you want to produce for this isolated period of time.

Of course it goes without saying that it must be written down and reviewed regularly. My good friend Wade Shealy used to record his goals on tape and listen to them every morning while he was going to work. It must have helped. He is an ace producer and has achieved some mighty high goals in his lifetime!

LEG TWO: HOW DO I INTEND TO ACCOMPLISH IT?

Answering this question will take a great deal of thought because this will be the *plan* you use that will determine your *procedure* to achieve your production goal. Your procedural plan needs to be carefully thought out and quite specific. This particular part of goal setting is important because this is what you truly have control over. You can't really control whether a person buys or not, but you can control what you *do* to try to generate those sales.

Many real estate sales agents have a tendency to shy away from a written plan of action because they think it tends to over-regulate their "free-spirited thinking." Their "independence" was one of the main reasons they were attracted to this business in the first place and they are reluctant to set guidelines that dictate what they must do. They have trouble understanding how specific daily requirements that they place upon themselves can actually free them up, as opposed to tying them down.

This plan of action is much like the rudder of a boat. If the boat has no rudder and wants to be totally free, then what are the odds of it reaching its destination? Won't it eventually crash on the rocks? Goals are the same way.

A production goal that does not have a sound plan of action will end up crashed on the rocks. Have you thought through how you are going to achieve your goals for this year? Have you crystallized this plan of action so that you know exactly what you have to do every day in order to accomplish it? After all, a production goal without a clearly thought-through plan is no more than a pipe dream.

Jim Wedgeworth shared with me the procedural game plan he used during his first couple of years until he built a strong referral base. In his words:

I always carry a little index card in my pocket on which I write down what I am going to do every day. First, I was going to make ten phone contacts. Second, approach three people cold about buying property whether in line at the grocery store or while walking around the harbor. Third, show property or give a listing presentation at least three times each week. I figured if I did these things every day, sooner or later somebody would buy. Even a blind squirrel finds an acorn once in a while.

The key here is that Jim had a plan. He planned his work and he worked his plan.

LEG THREE: WHY IT WILL BE WORTH THE PRICE?

The answer to this question serves as a real key component of the stool. In fact, if any one leg could be most important of all, it would be this one. The other two legs — *what* you want to accomplish and *how* you intend to accomplish it — are obviously important, but this third one is paramount.

If the first two legs of the stool are strong and intact but the third one is weak or rotten, won't it collapse? This third leg is your *purpose*, your driving passion that will carry you through all the obstacles, frustrations, and setbacks that you will encounter along the way. The deeper your purpose, the stronger your determination. The stronger your determination, the less chance you will have of being blown off track by the winds of adversity which always seem to threaten a noble cause.

It's this purpose of yours that will cause you to go the extra mile, make the extra calls, stay the extra hours, and close the extra time. It's this purpose that will serve as the bridge to carry you over the river flowing with fears of rejection and failure. It will cause you to pick up that phone and make that call, or walk up to the door and meet that person who is possibly trying to sell his own house. Your purpose is truly a powerful portion of your success in this business.

What is your purpose for being in this business? Did you quickly say "To make big bucks"? I'm afraid that will only carry you so far. You will not be able to achieve your true potential if that is your only purpose. Have you thought through your deeper purposes?

What truly motivates you? How do you discover a purpose that is deep enough to carry you through the frustration of rejection that you must surely face in this business?

It can only be found within yourself. It must be emotional, not logical. Back away. Dig deeply within your own mind and heart to determine what your driving force is. As within an atom, the power resides deep within your nucleus, which is yourself.

TRANSFORMING PURPOSE INTO REALITY

All right, you have now concluded what your primary purposes are. You have decided on your production goal that these purposes will bring about. Now let's talk about exactly how to transform these purposes into that production goal. Many people have achieved great accomplishments by consistently following these five steps. (I cannot remember where I heard these steps, but they certainly make good sense.)

1. Analyze
2. Organize
3. Visualize
4. Vocalize
5. Dramatize

Analyze. Every success requires a sacrifice. Before locking into your production goal, ask yourself a few questions and prepare yourself for the onslaught of emotional trauma while you are still in a reasonably logical state of mind. You don't want to decide whether you really want to be a soldier when you are in the heat of battle. Along with your personal questions, ask yourself the following questions:

- What amount of effort should I expect to exert in order to accomplish this goal?
- What sacrifices can I predict that achieving this goal will require?
- How can I maintain a proper balance in my life and still meet this goal?
- Who can I depend on to help me by serving as a support team to re-

mind me of my commitment and hold me accountable?

- What specifically will I train myself to think of that will keep me focused when I face opposition? (And you will!)

Once you have counted the cost of achievement by analyzing, you are ready for the next step.

Organize. This is probably one of the most difficult challenges for most real estate sales aces. I know it certainly is for me, and I know it is vitally important. Remember, this is the second leg of our stool, our *how* and our *procedural* goal, our *plan* of action. I have a sign with big red letters to the right of my desk that says: "PLAN IT! DO IT!"

It reminds me of what I should be doing and I am actually getting better at it! One of the frustrations that seems to overwhelm many real estate sales aces is the tremendous number of details and time requirements that surround this business, especially on the brokerage side. If you do not have a proactive plan to help you focus on where you should invest your time for the highest return, you will automatically react to whatever comes up during the day, and find yourself spending 80 percent of your time on the things that may generate about 20 percent of your income. What will generate the most income for you in this business?

THE TOP TEN INCOME GENERATORS

1. Persistently and proactively prospecting for new customers, both buyers and sellers (if you are in brokerage). (Also prospecting brokerage agents if you are an on-site agent.) Fall in love with it. Your primary tool here must be the telephone.
2. Following up on hot prospects by using the telephone or in person. Regular use of that telephone is far superior to mailing.
3. Keeping close communication and feedback with your sellers — your listing clients.
4. Contacting your past customers by phone, in person, and/or notes.
5. Following through after the closing to offer service above and beyond the call of duty (This is where many of your referrals will come from.)
6. Taking the next natural step by following numbers 4 and 5, asking for referrals of others who need your services.
7. Previewing properties. Know your product! Knowledge breeds confi-

dence. A good doctor knows what to prescribe to solve the problem. So should you.

8. Building a team of people who are willing to help you build your business. Make an effort to build relationships with the club bartenders, golf and tennis pros, and anyone who may come in contact with possible purchasers. You probably can't pay them, but you can sure remember their birthdays and major holidays. Don't try building your business alone. It's a lot tougher that way.

9. Starting a "brain trust" in your office. This is not a "bullshooting" group, but a good information exchange network. There may be three or four of you who work together quarterly on a newsletter. Share ideas, testimonials, and problems that you are facing.

10. Let's not forget appointments to present and list property! But then, if you are focused on the first nine ingredients, they will help you to build your business. "Build your business, and…they will come!"

Now devise a plan of action to determine the amount of time you will commit to each of these ten requirements for success. Naturally, there will be some alterations, so you must be flexible. But at least you will have a thought-through, written plan that will serve as a track to run on.

Visualize. What is visualization?

Does it mean seeing something external? That is part of it. The real power of visualization is what takes place internally, within your mind's eye. We have reviewed the power of words and how they create mental pictures. The external words we hear coupled with visual stimulation dramatically impact the internal state of mind. James Allen, author of *As a Man Thinketh*, presents the principle that "we become what we think about." What we hear and what we see, we think!

Many years ago, I spoke to a group of young college men and told them, "You will become what you think about all day long."

One guy raised his hand and said, "I don't believe that! That means I'd become a girl!"

Well, that's not exactly what I meant. I mean you will become in character what you feed into your mind and what you habitually dwell on.

The next natural step is speaking what we have been thinking. Be careful.

There is a tremendous power in the words we speak. *What you consistently and ardently profess, you will tend to possess.*

Vocalize. Saying aloud to yourself and to others what it is you are going to accomplish is much more important than you might imagine.

Benjamin Warf spent most of his life studying Indian dialects. After years of studying human behavior, he concluded that we think, behave, and believe the way we speak. There is a lot of truth in that. This explains why positive affirmations can serve as magnets for opportunities to reach our goals.

One of the most vivid memories I have of experiencing the power of goal vocalization was during the summer of 1972 in Mississippi and Arkansas. It was my third summer of door knocking. I had just graduated from the University of North Carolina, left behind my girlfriend Tillie (the love of my life who became my fantastic wife), and intended to put in my thirteen seventy-five hour weeks and get back home as quickly as possible.

About two-thirds of the way through the summer my sales manager, Dave Dean, spent a couple of hours with me explaining that because of the sales I had made so far, I had a shot at being one of the top salesmen in the company.... if I would be willing to stay a couple of extra weeks.

My immediate response was: "No way! I'm sick of knocking on doors! I'm going to finish up as early as possible and get home to Tillie!"

He just smiled and kept on selling. The one question he asked that got me thinking was, "Terry have you ever been the very best at anything really competitive?"

I replied, "No, not really."

That planted the seed of hope and challenge in my mind. Maybe this was my chance. After considering the effort this challenge would take and weighing the sacrifices such as not seeing Tillie and grinding through several more seventy-five-hour weeks knocking on doors alone, I committed myself to the challenge.

I didn't keep it to myself, though. Vocalizing this commitment to Tillie, Dave, and my entire organization of salespeople locked me into the enterprise in a stronger way. It sort of put my neck on the block! I put a photo of my main competitor on the dash of my car and every time I opened the car door (about forty times a day), I looked at it and said, "I'm going to beat you!" (Incidentally, he and I later became friends.)

By focusing on my crystallized goals one day at a time, and through a lot of encouragement from Dave and Tillie and with the help of a mighty good God, I finished the summer of 1972 as the number one salesperson. That year, the company had a record high of more than 7200 salespeople.

So, was it worth it? You bet your life it was! But it was also the toughest discipline I had ever experienced. And was what I vocalized important? Beyond a doubt.

Great challenges require great conviction, sacrifice, and total belief. Mohammed Ali was interviewed just before the championship fight with Joe Frazier. I have been told that Ali was asked how he felt about the fight.

He said, "If I win, a lot of people will be glad. If I lose, a lot of people will be sad."

He lost. That was the first time in recorded history that Ali had even alluded to the possibility of losing.

Dramatize. Ask yourself if you are a dramatic person. Whether you are or not is not going to make or break your success, but learning to dramatize the achievement of your goals in your mind before it happens will increase your odds of successful achievement.

By dramatizing, I mean you should amplify the achievement and prepare for it by acting "as if" it has happened. How would you act if the year ended and you were about to get into that new BMW? Act that way now. How would you carry yourself and talk if your goal had been achieved and you were planning the vacation of a lifetime? Act that way, talk that way. NOW! Visit your travel agent. Collect posters. Start learning the language. Study the culture. Treat it as if it has already happened.

Choose to lock into this attitude of *commitment.* In a world where the action behind this word seems almost passé, choose to be different. Be committed not only to your job, but to much more important things in your life. Commit to your spouse, your children, your family, your friends, and your own life. Be committed to learning to know your Creator, the one who made you the person you choose to become. After all, it is your thinking and acting on your thoughts that creates your own reality.

If you try to be everything to everybody, soon you won't be much of anything to anybody.
— T. L. Weaver

THE FINAL CHALLENGE

Are you growing up, or just growing old? Our world is filled with a lot of intellectual giants and an abundance of emotional midgets. Intellectually, we can send men to the moon, and make computers that can think clearly enough to defeat master chess players. But emotionally? That's a different story. Most people are still emotionally weak.

Most people are controlled by the situation they find themselves in. More often than not they are slaves to their emotions. This lack of maturity makes them ineffective as salespeople because it makes them ineffective as people.

Consider the guy who loses his job and then comes back and kills his boss and fellow employees. Or the young mother who kills her children because her lover didn't want them around. Or the forty-eight-year-old graduate student at Wayne State University who walked up to his professor and shot him to death because he was frustrated with math. There are a lot of emotionally deformed people taking up space and using up good air on this earth. Pick up any newspaper, any day, and you can easily find quite a collection of these nut cases.

These are extremes. But what about those of us who consider ourselves fairly normal people? What about the times when we let our sharp tongues inject the venom of anger deeply into the hearts of our loved ones? Or curse the backed-up traffic jam apparently caused by a bunch of curiosity seekers over a tiny fender-bender? Or when we slammed that club down after it seemed to deliberately smash a brand-new Titleist in the water?

We could go on and on, but there are two questions that need answering. Why do these episodes of emotional immaturity take place, and how can we change them? A psychiatrist or psychologist may have a deeper or more insightful opinion about this, but the answer I'll give is based purely on my observation of me and those around me.

Human beings are by nature self-centered. The two primary desires they tend to have in common are the desire for comfort and desire to feel important in the eyes of others.

William James, the father of modern psychology, once stated, "The greatest desire of the human being is not the sexual desire, or even the survival desire, but the desire to feel important and significant in the eyes of others."

I saw a quote once that went something like "The vast majority of the trouble in the world is caused by someone wanting to feel important." If you stop to think about that, it makes a lot of sense.

When we are self-absorbed and self-centered, if something interferes with our comfort or attempts to eliminate our feeling of importance we have a strong emotional reaction. That reaction can be focused externally or internally like an explosion or an implosion, depending on the type of personality.

How many times have our reactions wreaked havoc in our lives? How many words have we had to eat due to a decrease in our comfort level brought on by someone who ignored our self-importance? (I usually have my 'crow' medium well!)

So, are these desires for comfort and importance, in and of themselves, bad? No, just misdirected. A mind shift must be made. A grownup may determine that the comfort of others is more important than his or her own; he or she may determine that the accomplishment of the task at hand is more important than the feeling of self-importance.

In sales, you will meet quite a lot of resistance that can easily cause a reaction. You may experience irritation, anger, frustration, or even depression and despair if your desires are not properly directed. Some time back I taught (really forced) myself to say this: "I am not important, but what I am here to accomplish and the service I am here to provide is of utmost importance."

Over and over again, I repeated this phrase to myself. I brainwashed myself with it. Occasionally when I was dealing with a particularly difficult person, I felt a reaction bubbling up on the inside. I would think to myself, "Boy, it's a good thing I'm not important, because if I were that would really tick me off!"

One of the first things you must do to short-circuit these emotional impasses in life is to just decide to grow up.

Many years ago, Ann Landers printed an article that speaks to the subject. (I couldn't find the author but whoever it is has a keen understanding of this attitude that all of us should adopt.) It is entitled "Maturity:"

Maturity is many things. First, it is the ability to base a judgment on the big picture, the long haul. It means being able to pass up the fun for the moment, and select the course of action which will pay off later. One of the characteristics of infancy is the "I want it now" approach. Grownup people can wait.

Maturity is the ability to stick with a project or a situation until it has been completed. The adult who is constantly changing jobs, changing friends, and changing spouses is immature. He cannot stick it out because he has not grown up. Everything seems to turn sour or uninteresting after awhile.

Maturity is the capacity to face unpleasantness, frustration, discomfort, and defeat without complaint or collapse. The mature person knows that he can't have everything his own way. Life won't allow it. He is able to defer to circumstances, to other people, and to time.

Maturity is the ability to live up to your responsibilities and keep your word. This means being dependable. Dependability equates with personal integrity. Do you mean what you say, and say what you mean?

The world is filled with people who can't be counted on. They never seem to come through in the crunch. They are the cop-outs who break promises and substitute alibis for performances. Invariably, they show up late — or not at all. They are confused and disorganized. Their lives are a chaotic maze of unfinished business.

Maturity is the ability to make a decision and stand by it. Immature people spend most of their time exploring endless possibilities, and then they do nothing. Action requires courage, and there can be no maturity without courage.

Maturity is the ability to harness your abilities and your energies and to do more than is expected. The mature person refuses to settle for mediocrity. He would rather aim high and miss the mark, than aim low and make it.

Isn't it about time for all of us to make the choice to grow up, and not just grow old?

QUITTING — NOT AN OPTION!

Everyone who has ever accomplished anything of any great value has had at least one primary trait in common, the *desire* to quit. That desire is only an emotion, or feeling. And feelings can be overcome. But how? By the strength of will, which kicks in as a result of a goal that you are committed to. A true goal is born from the depths of your spirit where your creative power is found.

Many people seem to be like the kamikaze pilot who flew 188 missions. He was quite involved, but not really committed to his true mission. Many people tend to confuse activity with results. There is a big difference between being involved in something and being committed to it.

There's a story of an argument taking place between a pig and a chicken debating about who truly contributed the most to a great breakfast. The chicken was obviously making the case for the high quality eggs that she produced.

"Yes," said the pig, "no doubt you are very involved in the breakfast, but when it comes to that bacon, now *that's* what I call commitment!"

Why do we see so many people today give up so easily on a commitment they have made? I believe it boils down to character. I believe the strength of a person's commitment is in direct proportion to the depth of his or her character. It's a personal choice.

When the challenge you are facing seems almost insurmountable, when the "quitting demons" are pounding their battering rams of temptation against your mental door, release that power of will by reminding yourself of the vision of victory that will come if you refuse to give in — if you refuse to quit. Then, recommit to keep on keeping on — for at least today. Perhaps you can't hang on for a month, or a week, but you can hang on for today. Then repeat the same process tomorrow.

In 1973 when I was banging on doors selling books in Texas, I faced the toughest summer of my life. I had recruited a team of twelve people to go out to sell with me. Ten of them quit and went home within the first four weeks. My sales were slower than the previous summer. I had foolishly removed the radiator cap of an overheated car which exploded and severely burned my hand and my arm. Then I had been thrown into jail because of a real misunderstanding. (Can you imagine being put in jail for selling Bibles in America? Well, I *was!)*

The temptation to quit was making some mighty big headway! Then, out of the blue, a letter arrived from my dad. He empathized with my plight and told me about a time when he was discouraged in the banking business. He worked for a very tough, very belligerent, and ungrateful boss. One day when the bank auditors were there that man humiliated Dad right in front of the auditors. As Dad bit his lip and walked away, another officer of the bank who was a friend of Dad's saw the expression on his face and said, "Herman, don't quit. Let him fire you, but don't you quit."

Then he told me in his letter how much he believed in me. He ended the letter with, "You can't prevent the birds of despair from flying over your head, but you can keep them from building a nest in your hair." I couldn't have faced my dad as a quitter after that.

Persistence! That is paramount in this business and in your life. The pure power of your will is to fight against those tempting sirens whose goal is to dash your hopes on the rocks and destroy your potential with discouragement.

Think of that freckle-faced sickly English lad who was slow in school. He flunked the first grade three times. His dad really wanted him to go into law. Seeing how much his son was struggling in school, the father decided discipline was in order. A military school was the answer. The young man failed the entrance exam for the military school three different times. Throughout his life, he was a social cripple. He even suffered from a speech defect.

But to pass judgment upon this man's life in the early stages would be a serious mistake. How many people have ever impacted the history of the world the way Sir Winston Churchill did?

In the heat of World War II, Churchill was asked to address a graduating class (perhaps at Oxford). After he was introduced, he lifted his large frame and walked over to the podium to roaring applause. He lifted his head up, stood, and looked into the eyes of those young people facing the rest of their lives in some very uncertain times. And with the depth of conviction that only Churchill could have mustered, gave a speech that reverberated down the halls of history. Take note of his speech:

*"Never give up! Never — **never** — NEVER give up!"*

With that, he sat down. That's about as clear as it can get, isn't it?

Nothing in the world can take the place of persistence. Talent will not; nothing is more common than unsuccessful men with talent. Genius will not; unrewarded genius is almost a proverb. Education will not; the world is full of educated derelicts. Persistence and determination alone are omnipotent. The slogan 'Press on' has solved, and always will solve, the problems of the human race.
— Calvin Coolidge

You are to be congratulated! You have "pressed on" until the completion of this book, and you didn't give up. I hope you have marked it up, underlined it, and written notes in it. It was not written as a novel to be read through and forgotten. It was designed to be used as a reference guide to be studied frequently and to make a difference in your life. It was written to inform and inspire you.

Whether or not you take this *external information* and *inspiration* and *internalize* it into *education* and *motivation* is entirely up to you.

My hope is that you will make the contents of this book your own. Perhaps years from now you will look back on a successful career in real estate sales and, remembering this book, express your appreciation for it.

If that happens, all the effort will have been worthwhile.

MARKETING & SALES INSTITUTE, INC.

Terry L. Weaver, President, offers a myriad of training programs along with marketing and sales consultations and keynote speeches. For information about these programs, please visit www.MSIcorp.us.

MSI also offers two national conferences each year specifically for planned, luxury communities:

1. ACES© (Amenity Communities Excellence in Selling)
   - Meets each February.
   - Focuses on sales and management executives from planned communities.
2. Amenity Communities Marketing Summit©
   - Meets each fall.
   - Focuses on developers and marketing executives of planned communities.

Visit www.MSIcorp.us for detailed information.

MARKETING & SALES INSTITUTE, INC.
35 Boundary Street | Bluffton, S.C. 29910
Phone: 843-706-3872 | Fax 843-706-3873
e-mail: Terry@MSIcorp.us
or visit our website at: www.MSIcorp.us

To order additional copies of *Secrets of Selling From Real Estate Masters*

Contact: *MSI, Inc.*
35 Boundary Street
Bluffton, S.C. 29910

E-mail: Terry@MSIcorp.us
Phone: 843-706-3872
Fax 843-706-3873

MasterCard, VISA, AmEx